# Sarasvati

## The Cradle of Ancient Civilisation

Dilip Datta

**Indian Foundation for Vedic Science**
1051, Sector-1, Rohtak, Haryana, India, Pin -124001
Contact No. 09313033917; 09650183260
Email:vedicscience@rediffmail.com; vedicscience@gmail.com
Website : www.vedicscience.net

# First Edition

Kali era: 5123 (c. 2021)
Kalpa era : 1,97, 29, 49, 123
Brahma era: 15, 55, 21, 97, 29, 49, 123

## ISBN 9788194759331



Price: USD 7.99

INR: 250.00

# Printed by

Indian Foundation for Vedic Science, 1051, Sector-1, Rohtak-124001, Haryana

# Dedication

To All Those

who believe

Sarasvati Existed

Sarasvati Exists

And She will Exist in Future

# Contents

# Preface

In the ancient time, the Sindhu civilisation developed and flourished around the Sindhu (Indus) River. At one time that civilisation evolved and grew in size for reasons known and unknown. After some years, the people walked aimlessly in search of another place to settle, finally reaching the banks of river Sarasvati. That was the Vedic Age. At that time the Sarasvati river was wider than Indus, had strong currents and more fertile lands to offer. On the bank of Sarasvati, grew the Indus Sarasvati Civilisation. Till date, it is debatable why Sarasvati was treated with so much respect and worshipped both as a river and a goddess!

The change in the natural environment, perhaps the need of the Earth, created the tectonic movements that again moved the Aravallis centuries later, making the Sarasvati river either dry or lose its way into the Earth. With time the Indus Sarasvati Civilisation ended since the helpless humans had to move towards the other directions, mainly east and north in search of water and fertile lands to resettle, because no matter what happens in the world, life continues.

But then, what had happened to the Sarasvati river? Is it a lost river? How can a great river that helped create the ancient rich civilisation be lost?

Scholars are divided into two groups on this issue. One group deems it a myth. But the memory of the mighty river Sarasvati was preserved for four thousand years in India's oral traditions and in its scriptures. The river was not forgotten. Its memory echoed in legends, folk tales and names of places.

Hindus worship the Sarasvati like a mother. A symbol of feminine beauty, intelligence, creativity and basic rights; Sarasvati is a woman who is the epitome of knowledge, love and kindness. To this group, Sarasvati is the perennial source of energy, knowledge and water. Sarasvati is omnipotent and omniscient.

This book narrates the story of Sarasvati from two sources of information. One is mythological stories and the other is archaeological evidences. Reconciling the views of the two groups, the book has portrayed Sarasvati in three timelines with a belief that Sarasvati existed, Sarasvati exists and She will exist in future.

This book explores the birth of Sarasvati and her existence as the Goddess, the River and the Idol in her name. But I do not stop at this level. My research reveals that the essence of a birth travels through time and dimensions in other forms and life-stories. Hence Sarasvati who was the consort of Creator Brahmā at the time of creation of the Universe, reappears as Irshita in 6000 BC and reveals her presence in the present time in the name of Aditi.

There are perhaps more names. The book could have explored them too but I decided to bring out the essence of Sarasvati in detail through the stories, the struggles and the powers of womanhood in the ancient, the past and the present time: Sarasvati, Irshita and Aditi. On the other side, Brahmā, Rittwick and Arko define the different layers of male psychology through time and dimensions.

The novel not only illustrates the mythological and the real societies of the world today, but also delves into the connections of human sufferings, strengths and survival instincts of all times.

The novel explores Sarasvati's presence all the time. The amorous relationship that Irshita-Rittwik and Aditi-Arko share has traces of universal selfless love, which is contrasted with the relationship shared by Brahmā-Sarasvati. The novel circles around the idea that love has the strength of keeping on rooted to the true essence of life. Love can break the dimensions of this world and expose the past, present and future for souls that travel in search of the truth. Nothing is lost on this Earth, and Sarasvati is not the lost river.

# Sarasvati in the Ancient Timeline from Creation of Universe to 6000 BC

## Prelude

Supreme Lord Vishnu, the infinite reality and energy was sleeping. He desired and prompted Brahmā, the reservoir of knowledge, who emerged from his navel lotus, to create the Universe. It is not possible to create without obstacles. The purest form of creation forces time to circle around a life form. Brahmā too faced obstacles. He meditated and fell in a deep trance. The sound *'Om'* came from Brahmā's within and the Universe was created out of him. It started with an explosion through mental activity of Brahmā. Brahmā heard a sound. He looked around; nobody was there. Brahmā projected his big vision. And the Universe came into existence.

From *Avyakta* came the *Vyakta*, known as the Brahmanda that contained millions of Universes including Earth. The elusive forms of energies turned into the concrete shapes in a series of evolutionary sequences. In each of these spaces, Brahmā resided in different forms.

Brahmā was empowered by the Supreme Lord to do all the engineering work of creation in the Universe. Yet there was something missing. There was chaos all around. Brahmā was not happy. He saw everything was in a formless fluid state. He desired the need to bring order in all his creations. But then, how? He approached Lord Vishnu for His advice.

Supreme Lord told Brahmā, 'Each birth has two truths - one is absolute, infinite and immobile and therefore, not manifested and the other is Shakti - the definite energy, which creates the power of the absolute through vibrations and movements. So, you create Shakti to nurture harmony and introduce systems to the chaotic state of the newborn Universe.'

## The Woman in White

Brahmā started meditating again on his wish to bring the source of energy that would help him. He discovered the melody of mantra in the cacophony of chaos. The sound – waves of the mantra filled the Universe with vital energy, *prana*. And at that moment, a woman in white attire emerged from his within and came out through his mouth. Sarasvati emerged.

Sarasvati looked up at the eternal sky and the cosmos.

Brahmā said, 'A life is desired by a mind, but the life is conceived by the Shakti and then the life is formed. Yet there always remains obstacles. Without obstacles, no life can take its form.'

Sarasvati whispered and said, 'Knowledge helps everyone to solve problems and to remove obstacles'.

Brahmā nodded with closed eyes and said, 'I have created this Universe. Now you bring all the species and planetary systems in the Universe in order and create harmony amongst them.'

Sarasvati was sitting in a lotus position on a stone near the door of Brahmā's abode. She was in white with neatly tied hairs and no jewels.

She smiled and whispered to herself in her own meditation and said to Brahmā, 'Yes, it is true that you have created the Universe, but I will bring the present disorderly state of the Universe into order.'

Brahmā asked her, 'How are you sure to perform the hard task of converting chaos into order?'

'I am the goddess of learning. I am the goddess of speech. I represent the union of power and intelligence from which organised creation arises. I possess all the learnings of the Vedas, scriptures, and creative powers. I am the source of profound connection of fluidity-water, speech and thought. I nurture wisdom, fortune, intelligence, nourishment, brilliance, contentment, and devotion', Sarasvati answered.

Brahmā opened his eyes and saw that Sarasvati brought order all around. The cosmos acquired a structure and form. Stars spangled sky arched overhead, the oceans sank below and the Earth stood in between.

Brahmā exclaimed, 'I have gained the ability to sense, think, comprehend, perceive and communicate from your presence. I have understood that amidst chaos, there lies immense potential to create. I have become the creator of this Universe with you, Sarasvati as my wisdom.'

The sun rose and set. The moon waxed and waned. The tides flowed and ebbed. Seasons changed. Seeds germinated. Trees bloomed and withered. Birds migrated. Animals lived, ate and died. Life forms reproduced. Randomness made ways for the rhythm of life.

## Sarasvati, the Saviour

Gandharvas, the demigods, who sprang from the fragrance of flowers once stole the *soma plants*, whose intoxicating and invigorating sap was a favourite to the Gods. They wanted the plant back but were not able to figure out the way. Gods went to *Brahmāloka* and told Lord Brahmā helplessness.

Brahmā requested Sarasvati to take the situation under her control. Sarasvati took the challenge. She went to the garden of the Gandharvas and played her Veena. She played such an entrancing tunes on her Veena that the Gandharvas could not resist themselves.

'Teach us this music,' Gandharvas repeatedly requested Sarasvati.

'I shall do that, and help you to develop the skills for creating various Ragas and Raginis, only if you give back the soma plants to the Gods.'

The Gandharvas looked at each other for a while; they were undecided. But then, slowly they agreed and returned the *soma plant.*

Sarasvati smiled. She asked them all to sit. She told them about music - the sound of eternity. Once they were ready to learn, she said, 'Now be humble and answer my question'.

Gandharvas remained silent. She could see both patience and eagerness in their eyes. She asked, 'Are you prepared to accept the knowledge to play music?'

The Gandharvas looked happy and they nodded their heads in agreement. Sarasvati imparted them the knowledge of music. Thus, music was created. The Gandharvas became the celestial musicians, whose melodies and sense of music had more power to intoxicate the mind.

Sarasvati knew what she was doing. She was creating a gift that would last till the eternal flow of time. Music was the essence of creation, since the very sound *'Om'* was the vibration that created the Universe. She told the Gandharvas, 'Look, music has more intoxicating power than that of *soma rasa* and so, you are not loosing anything. You are gaining.'

Gandharvas realised that immediately.

By the time, Sarasvati came back to *Brahmāloka*, demons played another trick. Their leader started practising meditation to please Brahmā with the objective to conquer the three worlds. The Gods feared that the demon might receive a boon that would make him invincible; because Brahmā supported sycophancy and so, anyone could please him!

Gods had to come to *Brahmāloka* again to seek help from Sarasvati.

Knowing Brahmā, she agreed to a help the Gods. When the leader of the demons was in deep meditation, she sat on the tongue of the demon, and then applied her trick.

The demon came to Brahmā to ask for his boon. He did not know his speaking power was captured by Sarasvati. He thought that he asked for his desired boon, but in reality, he requested Brahmā to give him power to sleep all the time without having any urge to wake up.

'So be it,' Brahmā granted the demon's wish without knowing the role of Sarasvati. Gods were relieved.

## A Turning Point

Brahmā and Sarasvati became inseparable. Brahmā created and Sarasvati managed. Brahmā conceived and Sarasvati nurtured.

They were staying together in *Brahmāloka*. Years passed and life was normal there. One day, Sarasvati noticed change in Brahmā's attitude. He was, as if, stricken with the desire for deriving sexual pleasure. Brahmā was looking up on her with a terrible fit of sex hunger. Sometimes, someone's desire becomes a burden to other. This happened to Sarasvati. Brahmā's lust burdened her conscience.

Brahmā expressed his desire, 'You are the first woman in my life and so, let us unite.'

Sarasvati turned down his proposal and said, 'All that I offer must be used to improve the consciousness, not to indulge the senses.'

Brahmā could not control his amorous feelings anymore. He continued his pursuit and reminded Sarasvati each moment that she had to give up her resistance and accept his proposal.

Using his powers, he created three more heads so that he could feast his eyes by his four heads in four directions and see Sarasvati's beauty at all times. As a protest, Sarasvati stayed away from Brahmā. But, Brahmā was an obstinate person. To outwit Brahmā, Sarasvati took the form of a cow, but Brahmā chased her in the form of a bull. Sarasvati transformed herself into a mare, but Brahmā became a horse and chased her relentlessly.

Unfortunately, Brahmā could not catch Sarasvati in any of her forms. Such display of unbridled passion of Brahmā angered her and she cursed him, 'You have filled the world with longing and that is the seed of unhappiness. You have no respect for your soul, but encouraged it to nest in your physical mind. You are not worthy of reverence.'

Brahmā laughed.

Sarasvati continued in anger, 'There will be hardly any temple or festival in your name!'

Yet he laughed and undaunted by the curse, he created his fifth head on his trunk to cast his lustful gaze at Sarasvati when she sprang to the sky to escape.

Sarasvati was enraged. She brought the matter to the attention of Lord Vishnu and Lord Shiva. Everyone was quite disturbed to realise that Brahmā was violating the code of conduct and his actions motivated by desires, confined the consciousness and excited the ego and disturbed the serenity of the Cosmos.

Brahmā was, however, adamant. He attempted to touch Sarasvati. The news of transgression served to arouse Lord Shiva, the Supreme Ascetic from his meditation. Shiva opened his third eye, sensed Sarasvati's discomfort and in a fit of rage, turned into Bhairava, the Lord of Terror. He rushed towards Brahmā with blood-shot eyes, bellowing threateningly and cut off Brahmā's fifth head with his long, sharp nails.

Brahmā's passion was subdued but the fifth head that had got stuck to Bhairava's nails made him angry and restless. Bhairava was out of control to end the lust of Brahmā, but the Gods were afraid and they prayed to Sarasvati to bring the situation under control. Though she was pleased that Bhairava had come to protect her and acted against the misdeeds of Brahmā, she understood the situation. She called Bhairava with her gentle touch and brought him back to his gentle self. Peace and equanimity was restored all around.

Brahmā was quiet.

Sarasvati said, 'this is your own liberation from desires.'

## Brahmā, The Pertinacious Character

Brahmā incited by his lust, refused to give up the idea of acquiring Sarasvati as his consort. He played a trick

'I am going to perform a *Yagna* to cleanse myself', said Brahmā to Sarasvati.

Sarasvati was happy to know that Brahmā's consciousness had, at last, improved. She revealed to him the doctrine for his liberation. She also offered help from her side.

Brahmā was waiting for this opportunity. He said to her, 'In order to complete all the rituals required to make the *Yagna* fruitful,

I will require my wife by my side. Will you be able to be my wife?'

'Since you wish for a consort now and for a fruitful purpose, I agree,' said Sarasvati. Brahmā's desire was fulfilled. The two were thus reconciled and remained married for hundreds of years.

## Another Yagna – Brahmā's Deception

Brahmā wanted to improve the life forces in the three worlds. So, he decided to perform another sacrifice. All arrangement were made. When Brahmā was about to pour oblations into the sacrificial fire, the priest reminded him that the presence of his wife was necessary. Unfortunately, Sarasvati was busy at that time with some household chores.

The priest said to Brahmā, 'Without the equal participation of a wife in a Yagna, no advantage could be derived from the rites'.

Brahmā sent for Sarasvati. But she was not ready and was waiting for wives of other Gods to accompany her to the assembly: Lakshmi, Bhavani, Ganga, Svaha and Indrani. Brahmā realised that the auspicious time for the rituals were ticking away and he could not start performing the ceremony without a wife by his side.

He called Indra and said to him, 'Bring me a wife. I need to improve the life of the three worlds. Sometimes, we must focus on the broader issue. Managing the three worlds is a priority now'.

Indra could not find anyone. He finally brought a young, beautiful milkmaid to the assembly. Brahmā, with the permission of other Gods and holy sages, gave her the name Gayatri and empowered her to become the mother of the Vedas and the symbol of purity.

It was at this very moment, Sarasvati accompanied by the wives of other Gods reached the spot. Seeing the milkmaid dressed as a bride, sitting beside Brahmā and reciting the sacred mantras for the rites, she raged with anger,

'O, Brahmā! How could you marry another woman only for performing rites? You are the father of the Gods and holy sages. I am your wedded wife and I have supported you in everything. How could you insult my existence and make me feel ashamed at such an auspicious moment?'

Brahmā felt embarrassed.

He said, 'Time is a significant factor. I waited for you. The auspicious time for this ceremony was passing away. As a creator, I have responsibilities to impart life forces to the three worlds. All I needed was a wife. In your absence, there was no other alternative but to accept the milkmaid as my wife. I consulted all who are present here. They have given consent'.

Sarasvati could not believe what she heard. She said, 'You are trying to find ways to hide your own desires. You did what you wanted to do. And others supported you since everyone likes to explore more options'.

Brahmā came forward and said, 'I had to do this. Forgive this act of mine and I will never again offend you.'

Sarasvati turned to everyone and asked, 'To improve, to protect, to support the three worlds, do we really need to make such a random decision? Wouldn't such randomness create disbalance in all the three worlds? What would the creations learn? To abandon a consort and marry another, if needed, and that too at a short notice? Is the relation between a man and a woman so unpredictable and momentary?'

Silence prevailed.

Sarasvati's eyes burned like fire. She cursed.

To Brahmā: You will be worshipped only one day in a year.

To Indra: Your enemies shall overpower you and you will be driven out of Devalok bound in chains.

To Vishnu: You will face the consequence of Brighu's curse and will be born amongst men. You will not be able to endure the agony of your wife's abduction by your enemies and will live a life of a humble cattle-keeper.

To Rudra: By the curse of the holy sages, you shall be deprived of your manhood.

To Agni: You will be disliked by all because you will become a devourer of all things whether clean and unclean.

To the Priests: Henceforth, you shall be greedy and perform all rites, rituals and holy ceremonies for gifts and the quest for riches.

When the wives of other Gods tried to calm her and go back to their husbands, Sarasvati cursed them too.

To Lakshmi: You will never remain settled in one place. And you will be with people on Earth whom the other people and society at large will dislike.

To Indrani: You will not be happy with your husband's acts and everyone will look at you with a licentious motive. And you will lead a life of self-deception.

To the wives of the Gods: May you all remain barren and never enjoy the happiness of having children.

Everyone tried to calm her down, but failed.

Finally, Gayatri threw herself at her feet and pleaded to forgive her. Sarasvati in her another form of Savitri, calmed down and embraced the bride saying, 'A wife ought to obey the wishes and orders of her husband; and the wife who reproaches her husband and is quarrelsome, will assuredly go to hell when she dies. Therefore, let us both be attached to Brahmā'.

Gayatri agreed and said to Sarasvati, 'Your orders will always be obeyed by me and your friendship is precious to me.'

Brahmā, Sarasvati and Gayatri then lived together in the *Brahmāloka* merrily for many years.

## Sarasvati took the form of a River

Sarasvati's status in *Brahmāloka* was almost equal to that of Brahmā. She represented his mind, knowledge and intellect and was, thus, inseparable from him.

As the population continued to grow, many shifted from *Brahmāloka* to *Devaloka* and finally to *Martaloka,* crossing the Nisad mountain, Harivarsha and Hemkut as they approached the Himalayas. *Martaloka* became the second abode of the Gods. Supreme Lord Vishnu, Lord Brahmā and Lord Shiva shifted to the *Martaloka* in phases. *Martaloka* became the place of importance to all.

Time and growing population played a different equation on

Earth. As time grew old, the new lives thrived. Gradually the genesis of creation faded from the memories of the new humans. Yet it was the duty of the Gods to keep the flame alive. So, Brahmā and Vishnu called a meeting. They realised that a legacy can survive with the support of a perennial source of energy. In *Brahmāloka*, Sarasvati was equal to Brahmā. She too kept the life forms connected; yet when the Gods, Demons shifted from *Brahmāloka* to *Martaloka*, the status of Sarasvati gradually began to decline. She was, however, not only the Goddess of knowledge. She was also the perennial source of water which can help to create civilisations and keep the humans on Earth alive.

Brahmā and Vishnu knew that Sarasvati can perform a dual role with responsibility.

Before they could ask her to take up the new role of a river and reach Earth, Lord Shiva was woken from his meditation. He saw the three worlds overrun with corruption and evils. Lord Shiva decided that it was time to destroy the three worlds to renew the energies. He released a terrible fire, named Vadavagni that threatened all existence. Everything trembled. Everything burned.

Sarasvati observed silently.

Brahmā and Vishnu requested Shiva to calm down. But He would not listen to them. So, Sarasvati was approached by both of them.

Sarasvati told them, 'Lord Shiva burns everything that is impure and corrupt. This terrible creature will remain at the bottom of the ocean as long as Man is pure and wise. When wisdom is abandoned and Man corrupts the world, Vadavagni will emerge and destroy the Universe'.

Saying this Sarasvati left to meet Lord Shiva. She arrived at the ashram of Sage Uttanka. She met Lord Shiva there. Lord Shiva gave her a pot bearing the dreaded fire and told her to merge with a plaksha tree. She was then transformed by Lord Shiva into a river. She started flowing towards the plaksha tree and then to the ocean to immerse the pot of fire in its confines

## The Journey begins

On her journey, Sarasvati met Chitrangada, daughter of Celestial Viswakarma. She was making love to Surath, the son of king Sudas. Surath held her close and was whispering words of love. They were in an intertwined position. Face of Chitrangada was showing sign of eternal happiness.

Suddenly Viswakarma came there and saw his daughter and Surath hugging each other in an improper manner. Viswakarma became upset and dumfounded. He never expected this kind of behaviour from his daughter.

'How did you dare to love the son of the king Sudas? How could you cross the limits?' thundered Viswakarma.

Surath kept silence. Chitrangada moved forward to explain her love for Surath to Viswakarma. She wished her father would understand and accept them. In his anger, Viswakarma could not feel the pain of a daughter, of a lover, or of a woman. Viswakarma said to his daughter, 'I curse you that you will never get married and you will never become a mother'.

In the meantime, Surath left the place. Chitrangada expected Surath to take care of her. She waited there for Surath. Days passed. Surath did not come. Chitrangada was feeling helpless. She became depressed.

Sarasvati was so long observing. Sarasvati took pity on Chitrangada. She took Chitrangada on her lap. Chitrangada was carried miles away. She floated peacefully in the mild current of Sarasvati. When Sarasvati met Gomati at their confluence, She deposited Chitrangada to Gomati and proceeded further towards her destined destination. Gomati took care of Chitrangada.

## Sarasvati changed her Course for the Pilgrims

After a few days, Sarasvati reached a place near Kurukshetra. It was dawn. The birds were flying in the sky, the flowers were blooming, the butterflies were sitting on the flowers, the swans were floating in her flow of water. The environment was serene, as if, nature was welcoming life into a new day. She saw Rishi Pulastha discussing about something with his brothers seriously.

She became inquisitive. She overheard Pulastha telling his brothers, 'Sages of Naimishy Aranya had come to Kurukshetra with the aim to take a bath into the Sarasvati river, but they were unable to enter the deep forest that surrounded the river. So, they have made a pilgrimage site in the name of Yagnapabit just outside the forest. Many sages have come to stay there with the hope to take a dip into the sacred Sarasvati river'.

Hearing this, Sarasvati felt sad. She changed her course and began to flow westwards, forming many Kundas for the convenience of the pilgrims. The sages became happy and they offered prayer to Sarasvati.

## Sarasvati met Vasistha and Viswamitra

Sarasvati was flowing freely without any resistance. She was alone but happy. She was determined to develop civilised society settling along her bank. It was almost dusk. The birds were flying away to their nests. The sun was about to set. The sky was, as if, decorated with deep orange colour.

Suddenly she saw the great Rishi Viswamitra approaching her in a hurry. She could gauge that Rishi Viswamitra was in an enraged mood. He ordered Sarasvati, 'Bring Vasistha by your strong current and carry him westwards to my presence.'

Sarasvati asked Rishi Viswamitra in a trembled voice, 'What has happened to you, Rishi? Why are you so angered?'

Vishwamitra told, 'Vasistha had disturbed me in my penance and in the process, he had acquired more power. I will destroy his power as soon as you bring him to me.'

Sarasvati could not dare to refuse. She had to change her course again.

She went to Vasistha and told him what had happened. She also advised Vasistha not to agree to come with her.

But Vasistha agreed to flow with Sarasvati since he saw her helplessness. Such was the wisdom and strength of character of Vasistha. While flowing with her, Vasistha said, 'Oh, Goddess Sarasvati, you are born out of Brahmā, our grandfather and your auspicious water will be scattered all over the Earth. Every drop of water in this world is yours and we all are blessed by your grace.'

Sarasvati did not reply as she was worried for the life of Vasistha.

As soon as Sarasvati reached near the ashram of Viswamitra, he came forward to kill Vasistha. Sarasvati was taken aback. She did not wait any longer. She took Vasistha with her to other place. Sarasvati thus kept her words of two sages, but did not encourage Brahmāhatya.

This act of Sarasvati angered Viswamitra.

In anger, he cursed Sarasvati, 'Since you have deprived me of Vasistha's blood, you would carry blood and will be surrounded by demons.'

The curse came true. The evil spirits and demons started staying on the bank of Sarasvati river near the ashram of Vasistha. They started throwing unconsumed blood-stained flesh in the Sarasvati river.

No one could save Sarasvati from this distress. Finally one day, all the sages of the Earth pleased with Sarasvati's pristine truth, brought river Aruna and joined her with Sarasvati river. This ended the curse. Sarasvati's water became pollution free.

The demons realised their mistake. They requested the sages to free them from their sins. The sages said, 'We feel pity for you. For you, we create this place of confluence of the two pure rivers, Aruna and Sarasvati. If you take bath at this place, you can achieve moksha.'

All the demons took bath in that auspicious confluence and freed themselves of their guilts and sins. Then they, accompanied by the apsaras, went to the heaven.

## Sarasvati's status changed from River to Goddess

When Yajnavalkya lost his memory after being cursed by his teacher, he went to Konarak and performed austere penance. The Sun God was pleased and appeared before him. The Sun God told Yajnavalkya, 'Go to Sarasvati. Only she can help you regain your memory.'

Yajnavalkya could meet Sarasvati when she was flowing through a place near Pushkar. He offered his prayers by saying, 'I bow to you Bharati, the Goddess of letters, I offer my gratitude to you. You are the Goddess who herself is the explanation for all reasons. Your presence removes all ignorance. Your blessings save souls from doom. All great Rishis and Gods meditate on you and receive miraculous boons from you. Brahmā, Vishnu and Maheswar praise you for balancing the eternal peace in the three worlds. I am a mere human. Oh, Mother, I praise you from my heart and soul.'

Sarasvati was so pleased with the devotion of Yajnavalkya that she transformed her from the river to a Goddess and blessed Yajnavalkya that he would become a famous poet.

## Sarasvati allowed her Clay-image to be Worshipped

When Sarasvati was a little away from the ocean, a person who was dumb since birth requested Sarasvati to give him the power of speech. Sarasvati asked him to take a dip in the flow of her water. He regained his power of speech. Realising this, he was overwhelmed with joy and took some clay from the bank of the river and gave it the shape of the Goddess Bharati, having four arms with lotus, rosary, book and a pitcher. Sarasvati allowed him to pray her in the form of clay-image. The person, whose name was Ambuvachi, spread the new method of praying Sarasvati in all the places on the Earth.

Finally, Sarasvati moved with greater speed with the divine fire and merged with the ocean.

# Sarasvati in the Second Timeline 6000 BC to 1900 BC

## Reappearance of Brahmā and Sarasvati

It was in the year 6000 BC, a boy was born in the family of a direct ancestor of Karakarta in the Bharata dynasty. On the day of his christening, the head priest called the boy's father and told, 'This boy is destined to be a great Rishi. He will not look after your assets.' The priest gave his name – Rittwik.

When Rittwik was very young, he was, one day, going to take a bath in the river. On the way, he met a sage meditating under a peepal tree. He told the sage, 'I cannot sit long with closed eyes. I do not understand why one has to sit still for hours to attain power. What is that power you want to acquire by sitting for hours with closed eyes?'

The sage told him, 'Meditation is neither a way of living nor a process of self-elevation; it is rather a way to know our mind, body and soul. It is not power but peace which prevails. Meditation is the door to reach the realm of truth, which is pure blissful consciousness.'

Since that day Rittwik wanted to know the self within him and had a strong desire to connect it with the soul of the Universe. He began a course of asceticism. He brought his mind under control. He started practising _yoga_. He developed a belief that his existence was an integral part of the energy that the Universe emitted. He realised that prosperity was always the portion of a meek and humble heart.

When he was eighteen, his father called him one day and said, 'People from the Sindhu valley regions have started coming to our region. They have come in search of new occupation and settlement. Dear son, you as the son of a Karakarta, have to take the responsibility of expanding our region's periphery, increase our trade with the people of other civilisations and protect our people.'

Rittwik said, 'But I would like to find out who I am.'

His father said, 'Our people want to see you as their leader.'

Rittwik said with a smile, 'Well, my dearest father, I want to realise my inner force. I want to learn to be silent and, in the silence, I want to understand Supreme Lord's will and receive His force.'

His father said no more.

His mother tried to convince him to focus on family life but Rittwik said, 'I want to become a hermit.'

And he left home, and took his journey alone.

The path was not easy; it was a long tiresome passage towards an unknown place. Finally, after days of struggle, he reached the ashram of Rishi Vaswana.

Rittwik entered the ashram located amidst the forest. The ashram was beautiful. The Ashram had a calm and serene ambience. The place was surrounded by trees and thick *davana* scented leaves. Rittwik heard the sweet voices of the birds and wondered what breed those could be. He saw a few deer running around the place. He remembered how he had spent his childhood days, as a carefree soul in his father's land. He could have enjoyed his life with affluence by remaining as Karakarta of his region, but he decided to become an ascetic, seek spiritual enlightenment and remain a lifelong bramhachari. He was sure that life at the ashram would teach him the discipline and the truths about life. The ashram of Rishi Vaswana was a place that guided and guarded those who were walking the path of enlightenment.

Rishi accepted Rittwik as his disciple.

## Gurukula

When the sky was still dark and the birds just opened their eyes, and everything came alive, it was an auspicious time for meditation. Rittwik joined the other disciples assembled at a place in the *gurukula* to meditate in the presence of the *guru*. When the sun arose slowly from the horizon, they recited shlokas with their *guru*:

*saha naou avatu,*

*saha naou bhunaktu*

*saha viryang karavavahai*

*tejaswi naou adhitam astu*

*ma vidwisha vahai*

Rittwik kept busy the whole day with the work of *gurukul*. He was diligent and a good listener. He started practising meditation. One day, after completing his daily rituals, he sat under a banyan tree and closed his eyes. It was a moment when he was focusing on a few questions about life and its stories, he felt a shadow near-by. He felt tempted to open his eyes to see who was there. He controlled himself. His eyes quivered, but he remained still. And then suddenly he heard a commanding voice rebuking him.

'How dare you sit on the foot of my tree?' The voice of a girl startled Rittwik.

He opened his eyes. He saw a beautiful girl standing in front of him. She had flowing long black hair; and deep black eyes that reminded him of his mother.

He was embarrassed that a girl was chiding him. He was about to get up and leave the place, when she stopped him.

'You cannot leave a meditation unfinished!'

Rittwik nodded.

'Finish your task, I will do mine in the afternoon. But remember, this space is mine. Never dare to sit here again!'

Rittwik kept quite.

The girl left. But Rittwik could not concentrate again on his meditation. A question came to his mind. Who was the girl? He became restless. He felt something that he had never experienced before. He wanted to understand what it was. But something deep inside told him repeatedly that his days in the ashram will never be the same again.

## Irshita

She was unaware about the boy, who was watching her from behind the tree. She came to that same banyan tree and sat down. It was her time to meditate. She was wearing a white lace dress and was accompanied by a peacock and a swan. As she was about to immerse herself into the world of being one with the Universe, Rittwik stepped forward. He wanted to stop her for a while; he needed to understand why his heart had been beating faster than usual. Was she a deity?

She saw him, and calmly said, 'Take this rosary. You must meditate using this.'

Rittwik accepted it.

'Oh, you are wondering who I am!'

Rittwik said, 'Yes.'

'I am a goddess,' she said in a cold voice without expression.

Rittwik could not understand what she was wanting to communicate.

'Can you speak?', She asked, a little surprised.

Rittwik did not reply.

'Oh, if this is a trick you are going to have a hard time in this Ashram', She warned him angrily.

Rittwik looked at her intensely.

She said, 'I am Irshita, the daughter of your *guru.*'

Rittwik smiled.

Irshita continued, 'And why did you give up your luxurious life of a Karakarta in exchange for this austere lifestyle?'

Rittwik looked at Irshita, and kept silent. She felt a rush of warm breeze passing through them. She smiled.

'Come with me,' and she took him to see the first bloom on a tree that she had planted. She wanted to give him the flower but Rittwik stopped her.

He said, 'I am grateful for the lovely gift that you want to give me, but let it blossom there, I shall come and talk to it every morning. Would you not like that?'

She was happy with his wise words, but to tease him she said, 'There is no greater pleasure than plucking the flowers for fragrance.'

Rittwik said, 'There is joy in it but it is transient and derived from indulgence.'

She asked, 'Is indulgence a sin?'

He said, 'No, if it does not violate ethics. But life has other joys to offer, which are greater than those from indulgence.'

She asked, 'For instance?'

He smiled and replied, 'The joy of selfless sacrifice.'

She wanted to know, 'Is renunciation the only way to happiness?'

He said, 'No, not at all. You should do your duty sincerely without causing any harm to others. That is as great as asceticism.'

Rittwik's words created ripples of thoughts in her. She was happy that they met. She looked at him with admiration. Rittwik was moved by her beauty. And at that moment, he saw her enchanting smile and the dimples on her both cheeks. Irshita moved towards him, looked into his eyes and asked, 'Now tell me your name.'

'Rittwik.'

Rittwik, she thought, what a beautiful name!

## Temptation of the Soul

That night was different. Rittwik could not sleep. It was perhaps a sweet and happy time. The trees looked greener; the walls of the hut seemed to wink at him at intervals, everything around him transformed into happy and mystic dreams.

He stood up and went to the window. His thoughts were changed. He repented the feelings that he had nurtured in his heart for Rishi's daughter in the last two days. He felt, as if, the whole Universe was conspiring against him and the evil forces were overpowering him so that he could not achieve the goals of his life.

Rittwik wondered, where was he leading himself? His mind was like a pendulum full of fury and confusions. He said in a murmur, 'Oh, this is a life of sheer self-deception! I cannot control my mind. The very first moment of temptation is the first step down the ravine of sin. The thoughts that have encouraged me to grow my temptation are the steps of dereliction and fall.'

And without further delay he set out upon his task. He left his hut and stood silently looking at the vast sky in front of him. It was before dawn. There were no movements of trees and birds. The peace and serenity at the place made him to do a prayer. Gradually he calmed down. He remembered Irshita's words, 'In this vast Universe there is a language; it is the language of improvement, enthusiasm and love. If we follow that language, the entire Universe will come forward to help us.'

Her voice kept saying to him: 'In a state of conflicting mind and when vexed with a dilemma, one has to make a strong decision. The decision, which is derived from the inner being, guides one to choose the right path in his life.'

At that moment, Rittwik took a firm decision to become a pilgrim.

## A New Journey

Human lives revolve around journeys; sometimes journeys to new lands and sometimes journeys to their new selves. The movement involved is symbolic as without it, a human's cycle of birth is not completed. The Earth itself is moving and the process of movement involves millions of dynamic motions: the tides, the waves, shifting of tectonic plates, the days, the nights, the seasons, the birth and the death.

Rittwik was more interested in the journey than the destination. While leaving the ashram, he noticed the banyan tree where he had first met Irshita. His heart turned heavy with sadness. In the journey he saw beautiful sights. Green grasses looked like dancing in ecstasy, the tall deodar trees proudly poised to touch the sky, the birds flying towards the unknown. He felt that the stars guiding him towards some eternal ways that might have been travelled by many yet not explored enough. He told himself that he was born with a curse. He wanted to stop for some time and reflect on life's sorrows, but at that moment, he remembered what his guru had said, 'We all in some ways carry curses. Our lives are circumscribed by the chains of circumstances. Some are by the actions of our previous births and some are by the actions of our parents.'

Rittwik took a vow that he would not let the evil forces to capture him, though he knew that it would not be easy. He said to himself, 'The darkness of the new moon night cannot be dispelled by a few glowing fire flies.'

It was evening when he had reached a place that was quite deserted. There were trees all around. The open sky above gradually changed to a deep crimson hue. He could not see any locality nearby; only some scattered cottages and crops harvested to the surrounding lands. It was at this moment that he noticed a venomous snake crossing the road. The snake did not notice him, yet he felt helpless at the thought that he would not be able to do anything if any person would attack him. The thought that he had nothing with him, relieved him a little but nonetheless he was worried.

The wind was blowing. The sun slowly dropped in the horizon. The wind settled down. The stars came out and twinkled all across the sky. And then came out the beauty of the night sky in a beautiful copper shade. In the rays of the moon he saw a hut. He relaxed at the thought that he was not alone at that moment. No fear could touch him, since he had never let the evil overpower him with the negative energies; but being lonely was a devastating feeling which he wished to overcome.

He walked quickly towards that hut to find shelter for the long night. It was a village. He met a few people and politely connected with them, and asked for food and water.

Rittwik told them, 'I will spend the night at your village, and I request you to give me some water and food.'

An old man came forward and said, 'We were afraid of you when you entered our village, but now we see that you are a hermit. And we will provide you with food and water.'

Rittwik was relieved.

The next day he continued his journey towards the eastern side of that village and he passed several rivulets. And with time he became accustomed to the natural calamities, the natural life forms, and gradually all his worries about the snakes or other humans who might attack him vanished.

But hardships are part of life and he faced that too. For some reasons, the village boys did not like him and to keep him away from their village, they imitated him and threw stones at him. The local dogs barked at him. He wondered why they did not like him but then he kept reminding himself, 'Humans need to deal with their own unfortunate fates; they cannot lament for the troubles that come towards them in the forms of diseases, calamities and demises. Everyone faces life's traps at least once in life.'

In the journey, Rittwik had learnt not to complain; rather he strived to accumulate power to tolerate the nuisances that the villagers created to harass him. Even when the level of harassment crossed the limits, he remained quiet. He told himself, 'I must remain composed and take both happiness and sorrows equally as they come. There is no past, there is no present; I must try to reach the future. And this journey is to reach my destination.'

After a few days he reached a desert.

A striking nature of the desert was that desert demanded silence. In the ashram, life was a choice and one could leave it if one wanted. In the desert, that choice was invalid. Entering a desert, one has to follow the path of the sands without questioning. Disobedience in the desert means death.

The vastness of the desert made Rittwik look like a speck in the barren yellow sands. He remained silent. Being in the desert, it was a meditation. The only sound that he could hear was the wind blowing.

Amidst such a mystic moment he developed a power of intuition. A sense of collective consciousness wrapped him. He was no longer dependent on the truths that were taught to him by his elders and the societies of which he had been a part. He walked and walked through days and nights, as if, in search of something that he himself did not know. He never grew tired, he was not lost in thoughts anymore. Doubt did not come to his mind.

At nights he was guided by the stars. Surprisingly, whenever he was thirsty, he found something to quench his thirst. He realised that such occurrences were only possible due to the soul of the Universe. He told himself, 'When we want something with all our hearts and surrender ourselves to the Universe, we get close to the soul of the Universe and then we find everything that we need.'

One day, Rittwik witnessed the desert storm. There was torrential rain and the sands made it difficult for him to walk. A flash of lightning ripped through the darkness casting an eerie brightness all over the place.

As soon as the rain stopped, he could hear thunder somewhere ahead. He did not know why his heart got suddenly filled with happiness. He felt an uncontrollable urge to rush towards that point from which the thunder, that loud rumbling and crashing sound was coming. It was, as if, that sound was not a part of an ordinary storm, it was an invitation for him to explore something that he had been waiting for ages.

He ran like a mad man. And after a while, he came upon a wondrous sight. He stood motionless for hours. There it was, right in front of him. Yet he could not believe it.

The confluence of two rivers! In the middle of the rivers, there was a glowing white swan swimming; and sitting on that swan was a girl. They were floating.

He could not move. He wondered if he would be able to move again. When he looked into her dark eyes, he saw that her lips were poised between a laugh and silence. It seemed to him that time did not exist. The soul of the Universe surged within him and at that moment, he had learnt the language that everyone on Earth was capable of knowing and understanding - the language that expressed love; the language that transmitted vibration whenever two pairs of eyes met.

She smiled. The smile for which he has been waiting for since he was born as a human.

Rittwik felt exactly the same when he first saw Irshita at the ashram. At that moment, that girl on the white swan and Irshita became one to Rittwik's mind. He knew it and he longed to see Irshita. He longed to touch that girl in the middle of the river.

## The Confluence of two Hearts

Rittwik kept staring at that girl on the swan and wondered why she was floating in the river on that magnificent white swan. He could guess that one river might be Sindhu. But what was the name of the other river on which the girl was floating?

He took bath at that point of confluence of the two rivers. He felt overcome by a deep sense of peace as he sat on the bank. He slipped into a wonderful dream.

He saw Irshita coming to him with radiant smile on her face along with his father. Irshita came running and asked him, 'Why did you leave me alone? I would have been happy to bid you goodbye on that day when you had left the ashram.'

'I was guided by my consciousness', he said, his head bowed low.

'Your philosophy of life is meaningful, but do you know the pain of shattered love?'

He took a deep breath and whispered to himself, 'I am conscious of my faults.'

Irshita observed the confluence of those two rivers and without looking at him said, 'True love has the power to accept the beloved despite the faults. Such was my love for you.'

He whispered to her, 'I love you too.'

Irshita looked at him and asked, 'Then what did come in the way of your love for me?'

He smiled and said, 'What could I do? Love is a significant emotion of life that builds humans from within; but duty is the foremost part of life. Duty is the reality.'

'Variety is the essence of life, contradiction is its soul. The essence of joy and attraction lies in the variety.' She retorted. 'And don't you know that if you have left a life behind, then you would face conflicts within.'

He was silent.

'You do not know how to live life, so you faced conflict. Do remember that man's real enemy is not destiny but his own self. I have heard of the heavenly bliss when lovers are united. An empty pot reverberates while being filled, but the sound ceases when it is filled to the brim. It is the same with the hearts of lovers. When the hearts of lovers are filled with love, there is no room for words.' She said.

Whether it was a dream or a reality in another dimension, Rittwik could not understand, but he was unable to portray in words the eagerness that he had to meet and touch Irshita. The confluence of two rivers, the kiss of the sky and Earth, the desert - nothing could explain what was happening to him at that moment. Irshita was so near and yet so far. He sensed her presence. Her existence and varied forms haunted him: she was in front of him laughing, she was by the river bank looking at him, she was waving at him and laughing, she was calling him, she was wet when she stepped out of the river, and she was blushing and spreading her arms for him.

He followed her miles after miles but could not touch her. He could not stop her. She was laughing and walking away. Perhaps he heard her saying, 'Oh, you cannot reach me. You cannot touch me anymore.'

Rittwik saw everything vanishing. There was no one. That stream of one of the rivers hid itself deep into the desert. He was frightened. He forced himself to look more intensely and that woke him up.

It was a dream!

He sat still for hours. What had just happened? Where was he? He looked at the confluence. His face was expressionless; his heart was heavy with sorrow. The blue sky seemed to have descended into the river. Suddenly again the wind from the river began to blow, his sweat cooled and he was comfortable. The roar of the waves reached a crescendo. He thought again to take a dip into that river. And his mind transported to the river, and the river seemed to expand and contract.

He heard the waves of the river. He felt the currents of the river.

He moved towards the confluence of the rivers; and the more he went towards the river, the more he could see his dream distinctly. He felt as if Irshita had joined him and was by his side, walking with him towards that river. He looked at one of those rivers, which had suddenly vanished for a while and now had come back; its water was crystal clear. His eyes were focused beyond the point of the confluence, and he was mesmerised by a scene.

There it was again. Was it a swan? Was the swan playing with a lotus?

His mind, body and soul were suddenly filled with peace and thrilled with happiness. Looking at that elegant white swan, he lost himself. He murmured, *'Widen your consciousness to the dimension of the Earth and you will have a place for everything'*

## Situation in Reality

Rittwik's cheerful mood did not last. Clouds came. The swan flew away. The sky looked gloomy and threatened rain. The grief which was allayed for a while returned to wrench his heart as he remembered that the Rishi's daughter was herself to take vow of brahmacharya on her eighteenth birthday – and that day he knew had past while he had been in the wilderness of the desert. How could he now claim her hand!

With despair, he realised he had nowhere to go. He remained there for days, weeks... The nearby plants and trees with their fruits gave sustenance to his body. His spirit, however, was beyond healing. The birds flew overhead, heedless of him and his grief. His sole, silent companion was the swan who came to sit in the water opposite him. Even when he moved along the river and chose a different spot to sit, the swan would fly to take her position in front of him. 'She knows my sorrow', he thought, and he wondered, 'Has she too lost her loved one?'

Often he forgot his sorrow and prayed for the swan and, in his day-dreams, he saw Goddess Sarasvati riding on her, but the face and figure that the Goddess assumed was of Irshita. He spoke to the swan, talked to himself, and knew that he was raving, going mad, out in the open, under the hot sun and chill winds of the desert nights. But even in the blaze of the sun, he would not go far so as to remain close to the swan; and in the evening when the swan flew away, he remained there, for he did not know how to build a fire to protect himself from the cold.

Then came a miserable, desolate morning when the swan did not appear. He scanned the skies but she was nowhere to be seen. She did not appear for the next few days, while he sat staring into empty space in despair.

Rittwik kept peering into the sunlit sky, vainly trying to catch a glimpse of the swan. He had a fever, racked by mental anguish and pain.

Rittwik fainted

## The Rishi

An ashram was a spiritual hermitage, and a place where a system of education was nurtured in the bygone days. A *gurukula* was that education system in which the *shishya* lived with the guru, in the same house or an ashram in the midst of a dense forest. The relationship between the guru and his *shishyas* was parental and Universal. The *shishyas* were taught more about life and living. And the disappearance of a *shishya* was a very painful incident for a *guru*.

Everyone in the ashram became sad. They had hoped that Rittwik would come back. When seven days had passed and he did not come back, everyone began gossiping. The Rishi had asked himself again and again, 'Did Rittwik leave the ashram for his daughter? Did Irshita fall in love with Rittwik?'

The Rishi could not sleep for nights and then one night, he woke up and sat still. He decided to talk to his daughter the next morning. Looking at the vast sky above and the twinkling stars, he remembered Rittwik - a boy who was most knowledgeable in the moral, religious and spiritual laws among all the other disciples in the ashram.

The Rishi became restless. He kept commanding him to sleep. And sometimes he felt sleepy. Yet again, he woke up and looked at the sky above. The stars were moving and taking their positions. He observed intently: he saw Jupiter above the stars of Orion, near the constellation of Taurus - the bull was visible. He knew that constellations were used by people to relate stories of their beliefs, experiences and creations. Different cultures and countries had adopted their own constellations. He had his own beliefs too. He thought about his daughter, Irshita and his disciple, Rittwik.

It was early dawn. The Rishi got up from his bed. After finishing the daily morning chores, he returned to the main area of the ashram. He was lost in deep thoughts. He remembered how Rittwik had been well-versed in the ritual process. The Rishi was disappointed and worried because he felt that he should have understood the relationship between Irshita and Rittwik. The Rishi had told his wife that he would not insist Irshita to choose the life of a hermit. He got up and walked towards the hut of his daughter. He must talk to her.

## Irshita

Tears drop and fall like the dew, spreading emotions of joy and sorrow in phases of life. Irshita knew that nothing could bring back Rittwik, yet there was a distant hope in her eyes that often fell in the form of tears. She looked up at the sky. The sky was, as if, showering a gift of colours to her to ease her pain.

She remembered a voice.

Rittwik had once told her, 'The body and the soul are not enemies of each other; they are the two wheels of the same chariot. If one of the two breaks down, the strain has to be taken by the other. To torture the body for the upliftment of the soul and to devalue the soul for the physical pleasures are both wrong. The relationship between man and woman is like that of the body and soul. And love is so divine that each in love forgets the self. By sharing intense love, men and women can attain the heavenly bliss in their lives.'

Irshita had wondered why Rittwik told her these fundamental truths about life and relationships.

Irshita was sleepless in her hut. She had forgotten to eat. Those words of Rittwik kept coming back to her again and again. She was in a trance. She surrendered herself to the cool breeze that was blowing but unable to cure her depression. She stayed wide awake, staring blankly at the walls and the ceiling. And then decided to go out into the darkness. She went out of the hut and looked at the snow-clad peaks of the Shivalik mountains. She could not see much but the presence and silhouettes of those high rising mountains gave her much forbearance. In a moment everything around her heartened her in its own way. She felt that the ultimate essence of life was revealed to her and she thought, the easiest way to be happy was to cheerfully live the life given to us; to find pleasure in it, to experience the beauty and fragrance of it and to share it with others.

Old memories flushed in her mind again. She recalled what Rittwik had once said, 'Nature and man are inseparably linked together from the beginning to the end. In fact, they are twins. That is why life reveals itself in its true form only in presence of the nature. And then human begins to understand the content and the limitations of life. When human drifts away from the nature, life becomes one-sided. In that artificial one-sided existence, thoughts, feelings and desires assume unreal and distorted forms. I am fortunate that I could come to this *ashram*. I am able to see clearly the truth of life.'

Irshita came back to her hut. She had tears in her eyes again. She wanted to sleep. She could not. She drank water from the mud pot; the heat in her body evaporated and sweat soaked her. She went to bed breathing heavily. Her body ached on that bed of straw; and her mind yearned for Rittwik. She could not control herself and called out softly for her love. She decided that it was time to tell her father to bring back Rittwik to her. She needed him, even though he had left her alone, disregarding her love and breaking her heart. The darkness of that night pounced on her as she looked at the sky through the window and she saw the stars were twinkling brightly at her as if in derision!

*In love one cannot be powerful. In love one has to surrender. In love one cannot be angry, in love one has to be gentle. In love one cannot let go of lovers. In love one has to yearn for love.*

*In love there is no magic.*

## The Father and the Daughter

The Rishi and Irshita met in the morning at the ashram. They discussed what they each had felt and thought the night before. Both of them decided to leave the *ashram* the next morning and start a journey like a pilgrimage.

They started through the forest in silence, following the direction opposite to the movement of the sun in the sky until they reached the narrow road full of dust and dirt. After walking a long distance, the *Rishi* began to feel the fatigue. Heat was so powerful that even inside the forest they were feeling overheated. They continued walking. They reached a place where small trees were scattered here and there. There was an old abandoned well. They halted there for a while and ate some fruits.

Irshita felt that she could hear the sound of the Earth. For seven days they continued walking, climbing and descending the mountains, and each evening as the rays of the sun reflected from the tallest peaks, they took shelter either under a tree or in the hut of a family who gladly offered them shelter and treated them as guest.

Irshita thought, 'Travelling is like rebirth. While travelling one witnesses new situations, new places, new cultures, new languages. There are several barriers that one has to overcome while travelling to places unknown and this was like a new birth. Since the places are new and one is not connected to them, one sees only beauty in them and feels happy to be alive. The idea of being critical never exists in such a situation. That is why, a religious pilgrimage has always been one of the most objective ways of achieving insight. To explore a place is to explore the self.'

## Self-exploration

As they had been walking and had free time, Irshita thought that she would ask her father about some theological issues connected with God and humanity. According to her, for anything that happens in one's life, there is always an involvement with the God, but that is a complex one. Her idea about God was too simplistic and intuitive. Other person's understanding about relationship to God was based too much on concept, on intellect and on reasoning.

She asked her father, 'Does the God exist?'

'You believe that God exists, and so do I. So, God exists for both of us. But if someone doesn't believe in him, that doesn't mean God ceases to exist. Nor does it mean that the nonbeliever is wrong', the Rishi answered.

'Does that mean that the existence of God depends on a person's desire and power?'

'God is manifest everywhere. People first began to see God's hand in the caves and thunderstorms. Then they began to see God in the animals and in special places in the forest. But, in reality, God never ceased to live in the human heart in the form of love. Wherever you want to see the God, you will find him there. If you do not want to see Him, it does not matter so long as you perform good works. One becomes God's manifestation by becoming wiser and by living a simpler life', the Rishi clarified.

Irshita was listening to her father with opt attention.

'Many people say that the world that we see today does not exist. Is it true?' asked the curious daughter.

'Yes, my dear daughter. This world has a subtle and a gross form. Both the forms have come out of the Almighty who is of the form of consciousness. In other words, it is He who appears as the world and the world does not really exist. If, however, we say that it is real, then it consists of existence, and if we say that it does not exist, it still remains in the form of knowledge of consciousness.'

'Would you please clarify more elaborately', Irshita asked her father.

'You perhaps are conversant with the mode of cause and effect. Causes alone are real and all effects are unreal. Cause for everything is the Almighty, the Absolute which is Brahman. Because an effect is non-different from its cause, the effect has no independent status.'

The Rishi further clarified by giving an example of a cloth, 'The cloth can be divided into its threads. When the threads are taken out, there is no cloth to be seen. Thus, the threads that take the form of the cloth has reality and the reality of the cloth merely resides in the thread. If we proceed further in disaggregate level, we see and understand that it is cotton that appears like thread, and the reality of thread is not in the thread but in the cotton. On further examination, we find that cotton consists of atoms that are composed of the five elements. This means that it is in the atoms where reality resides. If we further examine these atoms by means of instruments, or even by the instrumentality of the mind, we experience a new concept. That is to say, nobody is able to know the origin.'

'Does such kind of knowledge constitute consciousness?', asked Irshita to the Rishi, her father.

'The word consciousness is among the most used word in both spiritual and scientific literature. At the same time, it is also among the most misunderstood terms. Yet consciousness is central to everything in life. An understanding of consciousness is important to understand life and creation, the spiritual journey and the evolution of life itself,' The Rishi explained.

'You once told me that one can experience his or her identity with the Absolute by the process of *sadhana*. Please explain me about *sadhana*', Irshita requested her father.

'The process of seeking and obtaining spiritual vision and inner transformation is *sadhana*. The process of *sadhana* is a human effort aiming at the realisation of higher values along with a sense of their gradation. This process of appropriate living and ascent to the higher levels is *sadhana*. It does not presuppose any fixed theoretic or dogmatic system of thought. It progressively discovers and reinterprets the thought process in the light of spiritual and cultural experience. *Sadhana* presupposes a general approach to life rather than any definite system of beliefs. The cultivation of moral attitudes is itself the initial phase of the process of *sadhana*. *Sadhana* means 'making'. It is the making of oneself, a process of self-transformation. That human nature can be transformed and raised above the shackles of greed, hatred and fear, is certainly the assumption underlying the practice of *sadhana*. By means of *sadhana*, one can connect with cosmic existence and its intermingling with the self.'

Irshita was absorbed with the explanation of her father on the issues raised in her mind. She felt proud of her father.

The next day Irshita and his father started walking again. After many hours, they halted at a place called *Pavibira*. The heat of the sun was unbearable. After this place, the green disappeared gradually and the barren lands welcomed them. The roads were full of rocks and there was scarcity of water. It was indeed a very difficult journey.

Irshita prayed to the God and thought aloud, 'I must find Rittwik soon, else it would become difficult for me to live.'

But many days passed and they could find no news of Rittwik. She wondered how they could find someone who had willingly disappeared in this vast land. Despite so many obstacles - mountains, rivers, forests, and the weather, she did not loose her hopes and enthusiasm. The Rishi tried to find people and sources who might have seen Rittwik. He was a handsome man and would never go unnoticed; but all in vain. They started thinking whether they were looking at the right place or not. There were hardly any humans dwelling. Only a few mountain tribes lived around the forests.

One month passed by. For a few days they had been getting a strange fragrance, and they tried to locate its source. While searching for that source, they crossed the barren land and reached fields of vegetation. There they saw a new kind of crop, and they asked the local people about it but no one said a word. It was surprising that no one answered them. The entire day they tried to find out about the crop. In the evening, they were tired. When they were resting under a tree, a woman came towards them and served them a drink in clay pots.

The woman smiled as they drank something sweet and refreshing. She greeted the Rishi and Irshita and kept pouring the drink into their clay pots. Irshita wanted to know more about that drink. The woman smiled and said, 'It seems you have come from a very far land! What is your profession?'

Irshita looked at her. She was young and beautiful. Irshita did not want to disclose her identity, but wanted to learn the recipe of that drink. Irshita thought, 'If I learn the recipe, I will make the drink and offer it to Rittwik.'

The woman was intelligent, she denied giving the recipe.

Irshita thought, 'Is the drink Somrasa?'

## The Journey Continues

Perilously, the expedition continued, through terrible storms. After a few days, they heaved a sigh of relief, thinking that their journey was nearing its end when they saw the valley widening itself and a wide river foaming down to meet another river. The Rishi guessed that it was the river that came from the Hindu Kush mountain range. The other river could be identified as Sindhu river. Compared to the torrential, forbidding grey waters of the Sindhu, the new river had clear transparent water.

Rishi saw change in Irshita's mood. Irshita looked absorbed in her inmost part. She appeared to be in a state of trance. She was, as if, not within herself. Suddenly, she, with an ecstasy of delight, said, 'She is Me, She is Me. I have to merge me with her.'

The Rishi noticed the look of anxiety and torment in her daughter's eyes. Irshita told her father, 'My dear father, I visualise now everything that happened in my previous birth. I am Sarasvati. That river with clear and transparent water is Sarasvati. I am sure that Rittwik must be somewhere around the confluence of these two rivers.' Saying this, Irshita started running towards the confluence. The Rishi started following Irshita.

They finally reached the spot where the sound and spray of the confluence of the rivers could be heard and seen. They found Rittwik there in a senseless condition.

Rittwik opened his eyes to find himself on a bed of dry grass with a fire glowing nearby, a tent above his head, and the Rishi's daughter by his side. He was sure he was in some heavenly realm.

When Rittwik regained his senses and saw the Rishi ministering to him, fear entered his heart. But the Rishi reassured him. 'Nothing should hinder you from loving each other; there was no reason to be ashamed of your feelings. Why should a man live without love when the Gods themselves cannot? Has anyone heard of a God without his consort?'

There and then the Rishi decided that the two should exchange marriage vows though the formal ceremony could only take place when the Rishi's wife and Rittwik's parent would be present.

## Rittwik's Parent

Rittwik's father, Karakarta received news about his son's disappearance from the *ashram*. The *ashram* was far away from the land ruled by the *Karakarta*. It was located on the top of a hill and very difficult to reach. But he was worried about his son and wondered if the powerful *Rishi* of the *ashram* had done any harm to Rittwik. He was his only child. Hearing the news of Rittwik's disappearance, Rishi's wife had confined herself in a room. Rittwik was a blessing from the Gods. The vast land area that the Karakarta ruled was very fertile but at times, there were droughts. After the birth of Rittwik there were no drought or famine. He was everyone's favourite. It was a difficult time for the entire land when Rittwik had left for the *ashram*, yet everyone accepted his decision because they loved him.

Time never waited for anyone. Two years had passed. Karakarta and his wife continued their search for their only child. They had grown old because of their grief, yet they made various pilgrimage to different confluences of rivers - known and unknown - to seek blessings for their lost boy. Once a sage had assured them that Rittwik would be a great man.

The very next day something happened. He was asleep when his wife came and called him early in the morning.

His wife smiled and said, 'Forgive me for waking you up so early. But I have news!'

He looked at her curiously.

She continued, 'Do you remember that sage who gave us assurance about Rittwik's life? He has come to our court with the news that Rittwik is alive!'

He could not believe what he heard. He did not know how to react. He asked, 'Where?'

She laughed and said, 'Come with me now.'

They both went to the sage and greeted him with folded palms. The sage smiled and told them, 'Walk till you find the confluence of two rivers. You will find your son there.'

They started walking days and night. Finally they could find the confluence of two rivers. They saw Rittwik with the Rishi and a beautiful girl there.

Rittwik begged that the marriage vows be exchanged by the side of the river. The swan, he feared, would not be there; even though she had been his sole companion in his misery and isolation. Rittwik wanted to be near her favourite spot to exchange the vows.

Suddenly Rittwik found the swan resting on a big lotus floating on the river. The colour of the water of the river was like that of milk.

Rittwik's voice rings out in joy. They were all happy. They started singing:

*'Though we behold not her face;*

*The Goddess is there too, yes;*

*Oh she, Sarasvati of ineffable grace;*

*Herself, yes, herself, comes to bless.'*

With reverence and homage, then, the river, associated as it was with the swan inevitably came to be known as Sarasvati; and to the people of Sindhu, it was the most sacred river and Goddess.

# Sarasvati in the Present Timeline

## A New Journey

Arko and Aditi had started doing work for their Ph.D degree almost at the same time. Arko's subject was physics; Aditi was doing research on archaeological evidence and its use to retrieve ancient culture. She submitted her thesis a year ago and got her Ph.D degree. Arko had submitted his dissertation in December 2017. Both are now finally relieved from the pressure of research.

Arko can initiate a job with strong determination but fails to complete it. According to his mother, it was due to his somnambulism. He is disorganised. He cannot complete any work in an orderly manner.

Aditi is different. She knows how to balance things in her own ways; a stable mind with positive outlook and absolute selfless, spiritual and focused.

Whenever Arko is in a difficult situation, she is there to help and set everything in order. Arko often tells her, 'You are born with high energy. You are optimistic but why are you impulsive sometimes?'

She never responds. At times, she gives a vacant look, and sometimes she smiles.

Arko, Aditi and her parents are discussing in the drawing room about the place where they should go for a vacation. Arko proposes to go to a jungle.

Aditi keeps her cellphone on the table, stretches out on the divan saying, 'Let's go on a Himalayan treck! It will be adventurous. We'll get to see the mystic beauty of the mountains. Besides, it'll be like a pilgrimage. We'll return totally refreshed.'

Arko had known Aditi since the college days. One day he was late for the class and hurrying up through the stairs when they collided with each other. She was not embarrassed, but Arko was, since he had fallen down. She calmly took his hand and helped him to stand up.

'What happened? It appears you are in a hurry. Can I help you?', She asked.

'I am late'. Then he rushed to enter the class.

The next day, Arko saw her in the canteen. She was sitting alone; he went and sat beside her. Arko was explaining to her why unfortunately he had collided with her the day before, but she kept laughing. On that day, Arko had discovered her. She radiated charisma and energy. She had a zeal for creating new ideas and executing those with finesse.

That was the beginning of a lifetime's friendship.

*    *    *    *

They reached Rishikesh by train.

This is their first journey. It is perhaps the beginning of many journeys together. There are anxieties and fears, but the presence of Aditi dilutes all the fears and anticipations of Arko.

Arko studies life through his observations and experiences. He believes that life moves at different spaces for different people. Life changes for humans over centuries, and sometimes, he has seen that humans often miss noticing the most important aspects of life. The change in nature and environment play a significant role both in the macrocosm and microcosm ways of life. Arko feels that life is a chain of events and it is upto humans to gain experience from those events. If one can learn to differentiate between good and evil and nurture positivity, then life becomes beautiful.

At Rishikesh, they join a group of young tourists coming from Uttarakhand. The plan is to travel to Satpancha from Badrinath.

The next day they reach Badrinath. From Badrinath, they take the route through the western side of Badrinath temple. They have a team leader named Lomosh.

'What a strange coincidence? The Rishi who accompanied Pandavas was also Lomosh!' Aditi points out to Arko.

Soon the journey started. When they reach Basudhara fall, two other people join the team. One is a middle aged sadhu and the other is an army officer.

'At this place many mythological persons practiced asceticism. Even Sree Krishna meditated at this place', Aditi informs.

From Basudhara, they proceed towards Lakshmiban.

'At this place, goddess Lakshmi practiced her asceticism,' Aditi tells Arko.

The place is very quiet and calm. There are *Bhurja trees* everywhere. The branches of the trees are white. The bark of the tree is red and flecked with white spots, like smears of sandal paste. On the opposite side of the river Alaknanda, just before the confluence of glaciers between the two mountain ranges, there is Alakapuri valley. On their way, the Neelkantha Mountain is seen clearly. From its peak, numerous streams of water rushes down its slope forming waterfalls as they leap into the valley below.

In the evening, they reach Chakratirtha. The colourful mountain peaks which are beautifully colored by the setting sun is seen from the place.

They see a lake shaped like a triangle. 'Skanda Purana states that three supreme Gods - Brahmā, Vishnu and Maheshwar sat on the three sides of this triangle and did their meditation,' Aditi narrates to Arko.

Up above is bright blue sky. Surrounding the area, there is a wall made of pristine white snow. The place is calm, quite and serene. Aditi and Arko get rejuvenated by this breath-taking sight and their tiredness of long trek vanishes in a trice.

*   *   *   *

At Managram, they meet a sadhu. He accompanies them up to a bridge. The sadhu starts narrating the mythological story about the bridge. When the sadhu declares that the river below the bridge is Sarasvati, Aditi, to Arko's surprise, starts shouting at the sadhu. She says, 'This is not the Sarasvati river. You should not spread rumours. What you say is neither mentioned in the mythological stories nor in the Puranas or in Mahabharata. In fact, I have not read it in any other religious book either.'

The sadhu being bewildered looks at Arko and stops talking further. After some time, he leaves the place. Aditi perches on a stone that forms a part of the bridge, and is soon relaxed. It is at that time Arko rediscovers Aditi.

'What happened to you? You seem to be in a different mood', Arko ventured to ask Aditi.

'History of Sarasvati is one of the most intriguing and fascinating episodes in mythology', she says.

'Sarasvati river does not exist any longer. It is lost.....' Arko argues.

'Nothing is lost on this Earth. How can a great river that nurtured an ancient rich civilisation be lost? Even if it is lost, it is still a glorious river in our mind. I love and respect Sarasvati river from the core of my heart,' says Aditi.

At this juncture, Arko developed an inquisitiveness to know more about Sarasvati river. He gets mesmerised by the way Aditi narrates the story of Sarasvati to him.

'See, if you want to know the genesis of Sarasvati river, then you have to be acquinted with four timelines. First, the period when Sarasvati was associated with the Creator of the Universe. Second, from the end of the last Ice Age around 11,000 B.C. to 6000 B.C. Third time line stretches between 6000 B.C. to 3000 B.C. And the fourth is the period between 3000 B.C. to 1900 B.C.'

'Now I know why our friends in the class called you Sarasvati.'

She smiles and says, 'And do you know what I called you?'

'What?', Arko is eager to hear something.

'You are Brahmā. Did your friends know that?', Aditi says with a knowing smile.

Arko does not reply. In that silent place, he huggs her and

kisses her forehead.

Aditi whispers into his ears, 'Let's go back to Kolkata, Arko. We have to prepare ourselves.'

'For what?', Arko is curious to know. He cannot understand the sudden change in Aditi's thoughts.

'I cannot continue this journey anymore. A journey without a purpose is futile!'

Arko looks at her and says, 'This is our break...'

Aditi stops him and says, 'I have dreamt about the Sarasvati river several times since the last few days. I don't know why I feel so restless. Sarasvati is calling me. I can hear that echo of her voice even now, she is calling me to find her. We must go to another journey soon.'

'What? Where?'

'To find the source of river Sarasvati and her course.'

Arko keeps silent.

'Arko, if you love me then we must go together...', Aditi requests Arko.

'Yes, Aditi. Let's go back and prepare ourselves to travel soon, to find the river Sarasvati.'

*  *  *  *

A river flows forever, being or non-being.

The folds of time carry the essence of any life if evolution promises to keep it.

And such had been the stories of most rivers since they were always the creators of civilisations on various parts of Earth. But Aditi has a different story to share. She has been waiting for long to express her inner experiences with Arko, and the day has come. Arko is waiting in the sitting room of her house, and she comes with tea.

'Look Arko, now that we have decided for the journey again, we need to discuss a few more things', she sounds serious.

Arko feels a slight tremor when Aditi's voice is firm; this could be either his heart or his sense of adventure, he is yet to discover.

'Listen,' Aditi makes sure that the listener is concentrating. 'Sarasvati is the mother of consciousness, who enlivens the inner beings. She is the symbol of harmony between the inner forces and the outer forces without which the humans will be in chaos, confusion and dilemma. To feel the presence of Sarasvati in one's essence, one must travel beyond the pleasures of the ordinary and reach the bare spirit of self.'

Aditi continues saying, 'Sara means essence and Sva means oneself. The complete meaning is *essence of one-self,* one who leads to essence of self through knowledge. But the name is also spelled in Sanskrit as *Surasa-vati* which means one with plenty of water. Water symbolises life and growth, so does knowledge and hence, Sarasvati is the quintessence of an evolved human soul.'

'Wait, do you mean that the other mythological gods or goddesses do not represent the human essence?', Arko suddenly remarks.

'And who is in your mind?', Aditi asks in a serious tone.

'May be the creator of this Universe...'

Aditi smiles for the first time since their conversation began.

Without answering Arko's question, she says, 'The Goddess Sarasvati wears only white saree and no jewels, which perhaps reflects her purity and state of mind. She sits on a beautiful lotus showing knowledge, light and truth; she has four hands symbolising supreme lord Brahmā's four heads, representing *manas, buddhi, citta,* and *ahamkara.* While Brahmā represents the abstract, she represents action and reality. Four hands hold four symbolic objects - *a pustaka* (book)*, a mala* (rosary), *a pot of water* and *a veena* (musical instrument)'.

'I know what they mean!', Arko startled Aditi.

She gives him a blank look for a few seconds. Arko smiles and says, 'The book symbolises the vedas representing knowledge. The rosary is the power of meditation, inner reflection and spirituality. A pot of water represents the power to segregate the right from wrong, the clean from unclean. And the musical instrument represents all creative faculties.'

Arko stops. Aditi appreciates Arko.

'Do you know how many Sarasvati temples are there in India?', Aditi asks Arko.

'I am not sure, but I know a few places: University of Roorkee, Pehowa in Haryana, Neel Sarasvati at Gairidhara, Kathmandu valley, Saradamba temple in Sringeri and Sarada temple in Neelam valley in Kashmir.

'Right you are', says Aditi to Arko.

'In Jainism and Buddhism, Sarasvati is known as the dispeller of darkness and ignorance, the remover of infatuations, the destroyer of miseries, and the bestower of knowledge. In early Buddhist mandalas, Sarasvati is located in the south-west of the innermost circle, between Brahmā and Vishnu, asserting her close connection with these two deities. She possesses many forms within Buddhism: vajra-sarasvati, vajrana-sarasvati, vajra-sarada and maha-sarasvati. In Tibet, she is known as vajra-sarasvati and is often depicted as wielding a thunderbolt. In Japan, the goddess Benten is seen as a manifestation of Sarasvati. Dai-Ben-Zai-Ten is the great divinity of reasoning. A myth in Japan speaks of a hideous pond-dwelling serpent that terrorised the villages and devoured the children for miles around. Benten could not bear to witness such destruction. She induced an Earthquake that made the serpent's lair vanish in the dust clouds. After a while she called the serpent, but at first Benten was filled with loathe. Yet the serpent king wooed her with tender and intelligent words until her heart melted, and making him promise to mend his savage ways. She married him. It is interesting to note that Benten, the goddess of speech was won by words.'

While describing about Sarasvati, Aditi fell into the trance of thoughts. Finally, she looks at Arko and says, 'You will never learn, will you?'

'Only, if you want me to.'

'I am not your teacher...'

'You know...,' Arko stops himself.

Aditi looks at him with curiosity. Arko looks back intensely into her eyes and whispers, 'Of course, you are my consort!'

They both laugh.

And somewhere the clouds rolled, the thunder was heard. The rains touched the lands.

*  *  *  *

## Present Time

Humans will never give up their objects of desire, until there is nothing more to be done.

It is almost the end of August, and Kolkata is getting ready for the upcoming Durga Puja festival, which is one month away. Places in the city are decorated with lights, pandals. Expensive pseudo temples are set up with care and excitement.

It is a time of the year when people of Kolkata love to visit Kumortuli. Aditi and Arko decide to go on a photo walk. They are accompanied by a group of young photographers, who exhibit their works in the Academy of Fine Arts each year. Both of them are very keen to get a few good photographs themselves.

They walk through the narrow alleys of Kumortuli, a place that looked like an ancient lost city of Gods.

'Only here they are made of clay and stones', Aditi whisper in her thoughts.

Arko look at her, click a shot of her face before saying, 'Aditi, why are you always so thoughtful?'

'It's my consciousness...' She says in a lost voice, 'I see her now in her form, draped in a golden white saree, with a swan and a veena. She is beautiful.

Aditi must have stared long at that idol of Sarasvati that is kept in a corner of the alleys. A little girl touches Aditi's fingers and says, 'Didi, she is Sarasvati. Will you buy her?'

Someone called out to the girl, 'Manu, Manu come here.' She

giggles and runs away amidst those idols of Gods and Goddesses.

Dazed and lost Aditi looked at the girl. She nods her head in a *no*, and holds Arko's left arm tightly. She shivers a little. Arko holds her for a few minutes, while her hairs touch his face; and at that moment, Arko remembers their past days in the university. Everyone used to be around her in the university because of her beauty and intellect. But she never looked around. In the library when she studied, people whispered around her, they talked about her, but she could never hear them. She was always in her own world. Yet, I was always there, silently observing her. And perhaps that is why she did notice me one day…

Aditi looks up. It appears that she is in the midst of a dream. 'Do you say something?'

Arko says, 'No. But what happened to you? Why were you shivering?'

'I don't know! It was as if someone was calling me. Someone who knew me.'

'Who?'

'I don't know.' She looks dazed again and stares at that end of the alley where the idol of Sarasvati in a white saree is waiting to be taken at some destination.

Arko touches her shoulder and asks, 'What is it Aditi?'

'Arko, we have places to visit. She is calling us...'

'Who is she? Aditi, look at me! Who is calling us?'

Aditi is in a trance. She faints into Arko's arms.

'Aditi! Aditi...!' Arko's voice trails away far from her and instead she can hear the words she had read from those old books in her grandfather's library years ago. Voices take over her consciousness and she is transported in a world where only Sarasvati exists everywhere.

∗　∗　∗　∗

Aditi is now resting at home. She looks out of her window and her thoughts wanders like the clouds across the open blue sky.

She remembers what he read about *Brahmāloka*.

There resided Brahmā and Sarasvati. *Brahmāloka* nurtures a system of collective marriage in which all women in a clan are regarded as wives of all men of that clan, and all men are husbands to all the women. Status is equal and all the children are regarded as children of the whole clan. There is no restrictions about sexual relationships and no hidden facts. No discrimination about this matter is allowed, no sense of shame or distorted views. *Brahmāloka* witnessed a very natural flow of life.

Aditi wonders why she needs to think about such freedom when she belongs to the present time and women are allowed to explore anything they want.

Arko sitting at the edge of the bed, is arranging some maps.

Aditi's mother comes in with tea and cookies.

Aditi's mother asks, 'Why such a sudden plan? Will the two of you manage such an extreme course of roads?'

Aditi asks without looking away from the window, 'Ma, are polygamy and harmonious society the same concepts?'

Arko coughs. Her mother looks at her and smiles. She says, 'Harmonious society is perhaps the best form of society but there is no existence of such an utopia.'

Yet in some other dimension or perhaps in Aditi's imagination a place did exist, where Brahmā instructed his sons to produce children of various categories: gods, demons, humans. And everyone lived in a blissful life without thinking much about the passage of time.

## Final Decision

Aditi and Arko had an hour-long discussion about the decision. Then they decide to travel once more to find the source of river Sarasvati in the month of November.

Their parents are aware about their plan. All the bookings are done.

Aditi is standing near the open window and looking at the sky. Arko goes close to her, touches her shoulders and whispers, 'Yes, we have decided. We are going to find the source of the river Sarasvati… whatever we find Aditi, I know that your soul will be set free.'

'Arko, it is not easy to find out the source of Sarasvati river and to know about her. If we are serious, then we have to get ourselves acquainted with three important issues. First, Sarasvati in *Rigveda*. Second, myths, realities and scientific studies on Rigvedic Sarasvati and third, Indus-Sarasvati Civilisation.

# Sarasvati in the Rigveda

## Prelude

During the Rigvedic age (8000 - 2500 BC), the word Sarasvati appeared both as a reference to a mighty river and as a significant deity. The Sarasvati river was said to have been discovered in 6020 BC by Brhamadasa, a disciple of Rishi Vaswana.

In *Rigveda*, Sarasvati symbolises anything that flows. It may be in the form of water or in the form of knowledge and wisdom. The name of Sarasvati is mentioned in all the mandalas of *Rigveda* except the fourth. *Rigveda* contains about forty five references to the Sarasvati river. One whole hymn is devoted to her.

Various Mandalas, Suktas and Slokas of *Rigveda* making reference of Sarasvati are:-

| Mandala | Sukta | Sloka |
|---|---|---|
| 1 | 3 | 10 – 11 |
| 1 | 89 | 3 |
| 1 | 142 | 9 |
| 2 | 30 | 8 |
| 2 | 41 | 16 – 18 |
| 3 | 23 | 4 |
| 5 | 43 | 11 |
| 6 | 49 | 7 |
| 6 | 50 | 12 |
| 6 | 52 | 6 |
| 6 | 61 | 1 – 14 |
| 7 | 36 | 6 |

| 7  | 95 | 1 – 6  |
|----|----|--------|
| 7  | 96 | 1 – 3  |
| 8  | 21 | 17     |
| 9  | 65 | 23     |
| 10 | 17 | 7 – 10 |
| 10 | 64 | 9      |
| 10 | 75 | 5      |

## Sarasvati as a Mother

The sages in the Rigvedic era had attributed their feelings to the Sarasvati river from the core of their hearts in the most respectful and adorable manner. She was described as the best of mothers, the best of rivers and the best of Gods.

While the sages chanted the hymns sitting before the pit for sacrificial fire, a kind of rhythm and resonance used to be created in the surrounding area with a vibration. This vibration helped to maintain harmony between their inside and outside.

Some of the slokas in the *Rigveda* praised the Sarasvati river for giving prosperity to the people as a mother does for her children.

*Rigveda* portrayed Sarasvati as an affectionate mother ready to protect people with her benevolence. She had innumerable admirers who praised her for whatever they achieved in their lifetime. Sages and Rishis explained various slokas in *Rigveda* describing the Sarasvati river with the deepest sense of calmness and patience.

In *Rigveda*, Sarasvati was the symbol for sanctity; the intellectual inspirations came from Sarasvati; She provided all not only with good food and shelter, but also with knowledge and intelligence. According to Hinduism, mother always holds a strong place in her progeny's life. In *Rigveda*, Sarasvati thus gets the highest place as everyone's mother.

## Sarasvati as a Major River

The Sarasvati river had been projected as the major river in the *Rigveda*. She flowed with her full strength loudly roaring and with strongly flowing water. The river Sarasvati was described in *Rigveda* as much bigger than Sindhu or the Indus river. During the Vedic period, river Sarasvati had coursed through the region between modern Yamuna and Sutlej. Sarasvati derived its waters from glaciers which had extensively covered the Himalayas. The melting of glaciers has also been referred in the *Rigveda* in mythological terms as an outcome of war between God Indra and the demon Vritra.

The enormity of waters available for agriculture and other occupations during those times had prompted the religiously bent ancient inhabitants to describe Sarasvati reverentially, as divine river arising from slowly moving serpent (Ahi), an apparent reference to the movement of glaciers.

## Sarasvati as a Goddess

Sarasvati was regarded as a Goddess who can give strength, food, prosperity and happiness. She was also worshiped as a protector from the enemy. Sarasvati had a fertile plateau where various types of grains were produced. Those who used to cultivate those lands and do farming, they used to acquire wealth. Thus, *Rigveda* had praised Sarasvati as a provider of fertile land. The goddess Sarasvati was originally a personification of this river, but later developed an independent identity.

## Influence of Sarasvati on Cultural Life

The Sarasvati had been to the early Indians what the Ganges is now to their descendants. When once the river had acquired a divine character, it was quite natural that she should be regarded as the patroness of ceremonies which were celebrated on the margin of her holy waters, and that her direction and blessing should be invoked as essential to their proper performance and success. The connection into which she was thus brought with sacred rites may have led to the further step of imagining her to have an influence on the composition of the hymns which formed so important a part of the proceedings, and of identifying her with Vāch, the goddess of speech.

Sarasvati mentioned in the *Rigveda* played an important role in Hinduism, since Vedic Sanskrit and the first part of the *Rigveda* were regarded to have originated when the Vedic people lived on its banks around 3000 BC.

The river Sarasvati is called Vrtraghni in *Rigveda*. This indicates that the river influenced the cultural life of the people living on its banks. *Rigveda* refers to ploughing by Indra on the banks of river Sarasvati cultivating barley, the earliest known staple food and one of the items used for oblation in the yajna ritual. Sarasvati was invoked to reduce tension and to cleanse the mind. Sarasvati is also praised for killing worms.

In *Rigveda*, Sarasvati is invoked in the ceremony of garbhadhana to facilitate and bless conception. The bridegroom was offered a potion invoking Sarasvati and Indra, the slayer of Vrtra in order to enable him to consummate the mirage. All these hymns point to the fact that the river played a significant role in the life of the people.

# Rigvedic Sarasvati

## Prelude

The forceful *slokas* in the *Rigveda* and many other references in other Vedic literatures had evoked interest in the minds of many sections of people about the Sarasvati river. They are researchers, geologists, archaeologists, historians and other scholars. They mainly wanted to know about four things: *existence, origin, courses* and *disappearance.*

## Existence

There are two schools of thoughts regarding the existence of Sarasvati.

The first group argues that a large river existed, somewhere in between river Sindhu and river Ganga of northern India. It had become dry in the course of time and finally was lost in the desert in a region near Rajasthan.

The second group opines that the present river system of northern India is such that would not allow any other big river as narrated in the *Rigveda* to exist. They hold the view that the Rigvedic Sarasvati may be a poetic depiction of the grand river Sindhu.

Advent of satellite imaging technology had, however, helped resolve this disputed issue. With the new technology, many interesting pictures of the area could be taken and the first group of scientists and historians, on the basis of the satellite images and overwhelming evidence from remote Earth sensing pictures, have presented their opinion in public as well as in professional forums about the discovery of the lost channel of the Sarasvati river. They further argue that the Vedic narratives about the river are not mere mythologies but are real and historical entities.

The first group of scholars argue that a large river existed prior to 3000 B.C. According to them, this river was as mighty as described as Sarasvati in the *Rigveda*. They say that climatic change and neo-tectonic movements caused migration and abandonment of several rivers and drainage systems. Some of them were lost because of the overburden of silt. But, several pieces of evidence left by these rivers have helped in proving the existence of a geomorphic feature in a particular location.

Be that as it may, with the aid of geological, hydrological and archaeological evidence and results of remote sensing through orbiting satellites, the mystery of the Sarasvati river is more or less solved. Geological records point to a period of aridity at the end stages of Pleistocene glaciations. This period gradually changed to a wet phase. At that time, when the climate became warmer, the glaciers began to break up. The frozen water held by them surged and began to flow downward. Such flows of water were supplemented by plentiful rainfall in the Himalayan regions. This gave rise to many rivers which flowed down to the plains in the form of waterfalls. Among these rivers were seven mighty river channels referred to as the Saptasindhu in the Vedic literatures.

The seven rivers are Sarasvati, Satadru (Sutlej), Vipasa (Beas), Asikni (Chenab), Parosni (Ravi), Vitasta (Jhelum) and Sindhu (Indus). Among these, the Sarasvati and the Sindhu were major rivers that flowed from the mountains right up to the sea. They brought with them enormous amounts of water and silt. The plains of Punjab, Rajasthan and north Gujarat thus were the most fertile regions. The area became a paradise on Earth. Scientists are of the opinion that it was in this land watered by the Sarasvati river, and its tributaries, a new civilisation— the Vedic civilisation of the Aranyas (forests) and Ashramas (hermitages) was established. For nearly six thousand years from 9000 to 3000 B.C., this civilisation based on agrarian economy had flourished.

This group argue that the ancient Vedic civilisation is concomitant to the flow of the mighty Sarasvati river and its tributaries. Satellite images clearly lay bare the existence of the Indus-Sarasvati river system from the Himalayas to the Arabian Sea. The scientists and geologists who carried out research on the geology of gulf of Khambhat, earlier known as Gulf of Cambay, pointed out to the existence in earlier ages of a large river flowing down from the north, and falling into the Indian Ocean somewhere in the location of the present gulf of Khambhat. It is not improbable that the river was Indus. It may be that the original course of the Indus from the Punjab was in a more south-easterly direction than what we find at the present time. Geological survey found a rock that appeared at the same level on the opposite sides of valleys in the Concan and Deccan. This gave ample proof of the existence of a river which was flowing east of the other Punjab rivers. Scientists opined that this river was Vedic Sarasvati.

## Origin

There is no consensus opinion about the origin of the river Sarasvati. Different scholars have different views. Most of the studies carried out till now is either on review of sanskrit literatures, or on Landsat imagery, or on field verifications in some parts of the Thar desert in Rajasthan, or on archaeological remains found at different places in Punjab, Haryana, Rajasthan and Gujarat.

The terrestrial Sarasvati river, according to researchers, emerged from a place called Plaksa. Plaksa has been mentioned in the Vedic literatures and Puranas. During the end of the last glacial period, around 12000 to 13000 years ago, melted water of one part of the glaciers started flowing from Plaksa. This place has been mentioned in Tandya Brahmana as Plaksa prasravana, the origin of Sarasvati. Plaksa was the name of a place having dense growth of Plaksa trees. Plaksa is today's Pilakhuwa or Pilkhana, located near Hapur in western UP.

The last melt-back lasted from about 9,000 to about 6,000 B.C. Scientists claim that Sarasvati originated at the time of the last Ice age. According to geological and glaciological studies, Sarasvati had originated in Bandarpoonch massif (Saravati-Rupin glacier confluence at Naitwar in western Garhwal). Naitwar is a village in Mori Block, 58 KMs north of Uttar Kashi. Some state that it originated from Har-ki-Dun glacier in Garhwal Himalayas. Again, Adibadri being located on the bank of river Somb, local people believe that Sarasvati originated from a place known as Rampur Herian near south of Adibadri. Adibadri is in northern Haryana. It is approached by road via Bilaspur and is about 2 KMs from the nearest village Kathgarh. A group of scientists argue that the Tons river and the Baspa river were the original glacial source of the Sarasvati river. The Tons river was one of the major Himalayan rivers and originated from Bandarpoonch.

There are mythological stories also. It is stated in Mahabharata that king Yudhisthir started from Kurujangala towards the north in search of a thick forest full of roots and fruits on the bank of river Sarasvati. After some time, he entered Dwaitavana, now known as Deoband. Deoband is a town and a municipality in Saharanpur district in Uttar Pradesh. Deoband is located about 150 km from Delhi and is about 30 km north of Muzaffarnagar.

There are further references to Sarasvati from Mahabharata. Pandavas proceeded towards Sarasvati located north of Marudhanvana which is now known as Meerut. These references indicate that the route of Sarasvati in the glacial period was through Deoband located to the north of Meerut. Deoband is located on the bank of the Sarasvati river. It is close to Himalayan hills and forest.

In the Skanda Purana, it is mentioned that the Sarasvati river emerges from a glacier and comes down to the Earth at Plaksa. In Skanda Purana, it is described that Sarasvati, while emerging from Plaksa, was obstructed by a mountain who wanted to marry her forcibly, which indicates that Himalayan range rose at least once on the course of river Sarasvati due to tectonic plate movement.

## Course

According to the study made by scientists, descending through Adibadri, Bhavanipur and Balchapur in the foothills to the plains, Sarasvati river took roughly a south-westerly course, passing through the plains of Punjab, Haryana, Rajasthan, Gujarat and finally merged with the ancient Arabian sea at the Great Rann of Kutch. In this long journey, Sarasvati had three tributaries, Shatadru (Sutlej) arising from Mount Kailash, Drishadvati from Siwalik hills and the old Yamuna. Together, they flowed along a channel, presently identified as that of the Ghaggar river, also called Hakra river in Rajasthan and Nara in Sindh.

River Sutlej joined Sarasvati as a tributary at Shatrana,

approximately 25 km south of the modern city of Patiala.

The river lost itself in the desert of Rajasthan while flowing into the Arabian ocean. This is further confirmed by the existence of the alluvial deposit at the head of the gulf of Khambhat. It flowed from the Himalayas through the present Ghaggar-Hakra bed in Punjab, Haryana, Rajasthan and Bahawalpur in Pakistan and then through the Nara bed in Sindh in Pakistan, making a large delta in the Rann of Kutch before flowing into the Arabian sea.

Sarasvati had passed through Bilaspur, Mustafabad, Thanesar, Bibipur and Pehowa and ultimately joined with river Ghaggar near Rasauli village in Punjab. Sarasvati and Ghaggar, are, therefore, supposed to be one and the same. A few scholars, however, use the name Ghaggar to describe Sarasvati's upper course and Hakra to its lower course. Some others refer to Sarasvati during its weak and declining stage by the name Ghaggar. Sarasvati having passed through many different kingdoms of India, had acquired many names. Upon reaching Kharjurivana, she was called Nanda. In the farthest west, it was known as Prachi. Jyotismati and Aruna were its other names.

That Sarasvati followed the course of Ghaggar through Rajasthan and Hakra in Bhawalpur before emptying into the Rann of Kutch via Nara in Sindh province, running parallel to the Indus River is evident from the fact that, in the Jaisalmer district of Rajasthan, even with very little rainfall and extreme weather conditions, ground water is available at a depth of about fifty meters. Wells in the vicinity do not dry up throughout the year. Groundwater samples exhibit negligible tritium content. Tritium is an isotope of hydrogen of triple mass. It indicates the absence of modern recharge. Independent isotope analyses and radioactive data have also corroborated that water stored under the sand dunes is at least a few thousand years old.

Results of tests carried out by Tata Institute of Fundamental Research at a place called Palanahas also confirmed that the groundwater there is about five thousand years old. Groundwater level in Kantli, which is a tributary of Sarasvati, is about thirty meters below ground level. Field investigations had shown water in that area possesses low salinity compared to its immediate vicinity.

The wells along the desert tract following the earlier course of the Sarasvati river do not dry up even during severe droughts. It suggests continuous supply of water from the upstream side. In contrast, the wells away from the old courses of the Sarasvati river have insufficient water and are mostly saline. Hydrologists have explained that such a phenomenon has been possible for the underground water remaining inside the old course of the Sarasvati river.

In the opinion of the scientists, around 6000 B.C., Sarasvati river having Yamuna and Sutlej as its tributaries was flowing along the Aravalli hills. Due to north-ward movement of the plate of Indian subcontinent, there was a tectonic upheaval of the Aravallis. As a result, the Sarasvati river kept on migrating towards the west and northwest. Its two tributaries, Yamuna and Sutlej migrated in the opposite directions. Yamuna moved east-ward to join with the Ganges later. Sutlej moved west-ward and joined later with Beas, a tributary of Indus river.

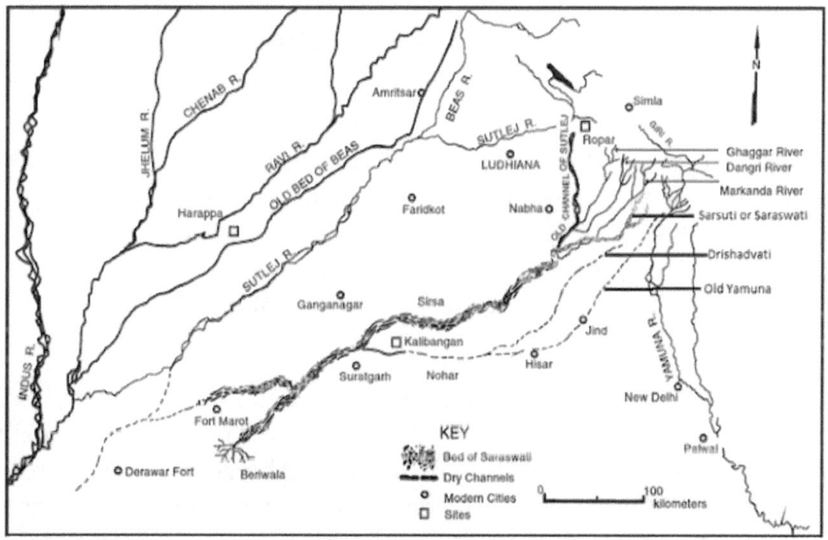


Studies of Landsat imagery revealed that there were mainly five stages of this migration of river Sarasvati. In the first stage, it was flowing along the foothills of Aravalli. In the second stage, it flowed through Bikaner and Ramdevera meeting Luni near Tilwara. In the third stage, Sarasvati passed through Jaisalmer and

Gad road. In the fourth stage, it flowed through the present dry bed of Ghaggar and Hakra. Finally, it flowed through Nara to meet Rann of Kutch.

There is a Vasishtha Ashram in Prithudaka, where Sarasvati made an U-bend around the ashram and became east-flowing. The ancient course of the Sutlej, after linking up with Sarasvati at Shatrana, did not join the Sindhu in the third millennium B.C., but had flowed directly through the Nara into the Rann of Kutch, as seen from a palaeo-channel on the Landsat imagery.

There is a palaeo-channel south-east of river Markanda; Chautang joins the Ghaggar near Suratgarh, Ghaggar bifurcates near Anupgarh and both palaeo-channels end abruptly. Many channels of dried-up river beds are found in the satellite images of north-west India. There was an east-ward shift of the channels of the Yamuna and a west-ward shift of the channels of the Sutlej. All these channels were flowing into the Sarasvati in the third millennium B.C. Many dry river beds are found between Yamuna and Sutlej. These are the beds which moved east-ward disconnecting from Sarasvati. The eastern arm of the Hakra is formed by four rivers – the Chautang or Drishadvati, the Sarasvati, the Ghaggar and the Wah or Sonamwal. The western arm of Hakra is formed by three rivers known as Naiwal.

Geographically, the Sarasvati basin has been traced by the scientist to the currently known Ghaggar-Hakra-Raini-Nara-Wahinda-Mihran-Puran channels. They say that Ghaggar might have been a stream that emerged from the rise of the Siwaliks and subsequently joined with Sarasvati. This network runs parallel to the Indus across Sind.

With the help of the images taken in 1972, the scientists have traced that the wide valley of the Sarasvati river ran from Suratgarh through Anupgarh to Fort Abbas and Ahmadpur East. From Anupgarh another wide belt of discontinuous patches of dark grey tone runs south-west-ward upto Sakhi. From Sakhi, the remnant of the former valley can be traced towards the west. The imagery reveals the presence of a narrow zone of saline fields, partly obliterated by the overlying sand dunes, extending upto Khangarh. To the south of Khangarh, a narrow strip of green vegetation, producing a slightly darker tone than the surroundings, have been identified. It runs from Islamgarh, through DharmiKhu, Ghantial, Shahgarh, Babuwali and Rajar to Mihal Mungra. The scientists claim that this was the course of the Sarasvati from the Himalaya to the Rann of Kutch.

## Disappearance

According to the scientists, Sarasvati river got dried up due to the diversion of the course of both Sutlej and Yamuna. The groundwater and geophysical data corroborates these findings. The presence of older alluvial plains with medium textured soils below the sands of Thar Desert indicates activities of some mighty rivers in the past. The geophysical surveys in Ganganagar, Bikaner and Jaisalmer areas have revealed several zones of less saline underground water which is dated more than five thousand years old.

Another group of geologists claim that, when Sutlej changed its course to the west-ward and abandoned the east arm of Hakra, the Sarasvati was left in the possession of the deserted channel in the sands of which its waters were swallowed up. Some geologists and archaeologists claim that a long and devastating drought caused the drying up of Sarasvati.

The National Geophysical Research Institute called out evidence of twelve Earthquakes from archaeological and geomorphologic records of excavated Harappan sites. The Institute has concluded that an Earthquake around 3100 B.C. may have resulted in Sarasvati losing Yamuna.

Scientists also refer to an Earthquake in 2500 B.C., when Sarasvati might have lost Sutlej which moved west-ward. The drying up of the Sarasvati river around 1900 B.C. was confirmed archaeologically. Due to major tectonic plate movements and shifts in the Earth's crust, Sutlej river and the Drishadvati river, the two tributaries of Sarasvati were captured by other rivers. This was the main reason for drying up of Sarasvati.

Some scientists consider that Sarasvati river was alive in Kalibangan in the third millennium B.C. and dried up at the turn of the second millennium. Archaeological evidence also found that Sutlej river was the main tributary of the Sarasvati. Its deviation from the Sarasvati and subsequent joining with the Beas was the principal factor that caused the Sarasvati to be deprived of much of its water input and thereby go dry.

Some recent studies suggest that drying up of the Sarasvati river might have been accelerated due to natural solar cycles or due to manmade causes very much like the present-day climate change. Deforestation and urbanisation is likely to have been a contributing cause of climate change and this must have taken place in Indus Sarasvati valley civilisation because of increasing needs of agricultural products.

# Indus-Sarasvati Civilisation

## Prelude

Indus-Sarasvati civilisation might have started in the Indian subcontinent between 3500 to 3000 B.C. The civilisation was based on river centric economy. Fertile soil of the river systems had helped it to grow. Trading business had grown to a large extent. This led to expansion of urbanisation. The earliest evidence of such urbanisation was found around 3000 BC in the valley located between Indus river and Sarasvati river. Many great cities, namely, Mohenjadaro, Harappa, Lothal, Dholavira, Kalibangan, Kot Diji (Sind), Rupar, Rakhigarhi, Banawali, Mitathal, Surkotada, Ganweriwala (Bahawalpur) and Bhagatrāv were the centers of this civilisation.

The area that witnessed this civilisation was vast. In the east was Alamgirpur in the upper Ganga-Yamuna doab. In the west was Sutkagen-dor on the sea-board of south Baluchistan. In the north was Ropar, almost impinging upon the sub-Himalayan foothills. In the south was Bhagatrāv, on the estuary of the Kim, a small river between the Narmada and Tapti. From the east to west, the civilisation covered an area of about 1,600 kilometres, and from north to south, area was about 1,100 kilometres.

The survey conducted by the scientists mapped out a total of 414 archaeological sites on the bed of Indus and Sarasvati river where a society had grown with developed economy. Satellite photos and ground surveys confirmed that Sarasvati river was at that time a mighty river whose water flow was much more than that of Indus. The importance of Sarasvati river can be gauged from the fact that there were far more settlements clustered around the course of Sarasvati than along the Indus. With this background, the scientists and researchers involved in this survey adopted the term Indus-Sarasvati Civilisation (ISC) instead of Indus-Valley Civilisation (IVC).

The reason for the change in nomenclature lies in the most startling archaeological discoveries made during the last two and a half decades by two scientists, namely, Rafique Mughal and S. P. Gupta. These discoveries were made in that part of the lost Sarasvati basin which lies in Cholistan deserts of Bikaner located in the Bahawalpur region of Pakistan, adjoining north-western Rajasthan. This has now firmly established the primacy of the Sarasvati river over the Indus in terms of concentration of the sites of different categories. Rafique Mughal has found the remains of as many as 363 sites in Bahawalpur of this civilisation. His conclusions were supported by similar discoveries made in India. J. P. Joshi, I. D. Divedi, R. S. Bisht, A. Nath, Suraj Bhan and others have discovered around 250 sites in the basin of the Sarasvati and its several tributaries such as the Drishadvati, in north-eastern Rajasthan, Haryana and western Uttar Pradesh. Thus, there appears to be more than 1200 Harappan sites on the Sarasvati and its tributaries in India and Pakistan. And certainly there are many more awaiting the investigations of archaeologists. On the other hand, there are about 150 sites on the Indus and its tributaries.

The Indus and the Sarasvati together played the same role in the making of the Bronze Age South Asian Civilisation which the Tigris and Euphrates played in the making of the Mesopotamian Civilisation during the same period. The Indus-Sarasvati Civilisation was, according to the scientists, around four times more in area-coverage than any contemporary civilisation, including Egyptian and Mesopotamian.

## Growth of the Indus-Sarasvati Civilisation

Civilisation begins to appear when a workable system for living, that is proper relationship between man and nature, is established in accordance with the features of a given region. In Saptasindhu, the land of the seven rivers, the axis was the mighty Sarasvati river flowing from the mountains to the ocean.

In the opinion of some scholars, clusters of people settled along the Nile, Euphrates and Tigris rivers started moving towards Indus and Sarasvati rivers in the Indian subcontinent by 4500 B.C. This was probably due to heavy floods followed by desiccation in the settled locations around those three rivers. Growth of population disproportionate to availability of food was also one of the reasons of migration.

Thereafter, the stage was set for the next big step in the history of human civilisation in the Indian subcontinent along Indus and Sarasvati rivers and their tributaries.

This is what was expected. There was not one single instance of any civilisation which had grown spontaneously. There was not a race in the world which became civilised unless another civilised race came and mingled with that race. The origin of civilisation must have belonged, so to say, to one or two races who went abroad, propagated their ideas, and intermingled with other races and thus civilisation expanded. All civilisations grew that way. One wave of a race had gone from its birthplace to a distant land and made a wonderful civilisation. A certain race became civilised. They came and conquered another race. They brought better blood, stronger physiques. They took up the mind of the conquered race and added that to their body and pushed civilisation still further.

## River-system

The Indus-Sarasvati Civilisation would not have flourished had the agricultural lands not been watered by a vast stretch of a river system. The seven rivers mainly contributed to keep the river system unimpeded. They were Satudri (Sutlej), Vipas (Beas), Parushni (Ravi), Asikini (Chenab), Vitasta (Jhelum), Sindhu (Indus) and Sarasvati. These rivers were so well distributed that a vast area of valleys became very fertile producing principal crops, namely, wheat, barley and cotton.

## Mode of living

The ancient Indo-Aryans had lived on agriculture and animal husbandry. Animals were both domesticated and wild. There is also evidence of the domestication of cats, dogs, and perhaps elephants. The data about the camel and horse are less conclusive.

There is evidence to show that the people used to eat cereals, vegetables, fruits, fish, fowl, mutton, beef, and pork. Staple foods were based on rice, wheat and barley. Rice was not a popular food. The use of medicines was rare, though when needed they used herbal medicines. Water transportation by boats and ships as means of conveyance was popular. Besides, bullock-carts were also used. During this period, Rigvedic people not only knew the sea but were mariners and had trade relations with the outside world.

The population of the cities was a cosmopolitan one. It might have included mediterraneans, proto-australoids, alpines, and mongoloids. In keeping with such a mixed population, there was a wide variety of religious practices. Urbanisation was the main feature of Indus-Sarasvati Civilisation. Nomad pastoralists and agricultural settlement were the mainstreamers. As regards the language spoken at that time, scholars opine that they used to speak in Proto Indo European language. This language got transformed into Vedic language, which later developed into Sanskrit. The religio-philosophical thoughts that developed in the north-western part of the Indian subcontinent, which is today's Pakistan, formed a unitary culture in the fourth millennium B.C.

They knew about the technology for building, metallurgy and the tools necessary for their use, arts and crafts. Materials used for construction of houses were metal, stone, mud and wood and brick, which is the principal material for houses in Indus-Sarasvati Civilisation.

During Indus-Sarasvati Civilisation, cotton plants were extensively cultivated and cotton fabric was exported. Weaving with loom and shuttle was common. Processes and techniques used for weaving and metallurgy were of higher nature and grade. Fixed brick-altars or hearths were very common in Indus-Sarasvati Civilisation.

## Dress

Not much evidence is available regarding the dress of the Indus people. The portrayal of a man on a potsherd from Harappa shows the use of dhoti. Use of shawl as an upper garment is indicated by the famous picture of a priest from Mohenjodaro. The use of dhoti and shawl brings to mind the picture of an average Hindu of the modern Indian village. The evidence of sewing needles and buttons shows that the people were used to stitch clothes. The hair dressing styles of women and adornment of men-folk suggest that a section of the population was rich and lived a luxurious life. They were used to wear ornaments from head to foot. Ear-rings, necklaces, bracelets, girdles and anklets were common. Use of gold, silver and copper in Indus Sarasvati Civilisation was very common.

## Religion

Their religion was based on many deities who they believed as manifestations of one primal cause. This shows their attempt to penetrate the mysteries of nature. They were also eager to know the reasons for the cycle of life and death. They realised that there were unseen causes behind the observable phenomena.

## Class Structure

Sarasvati river, which was a mighty river gave sustenance to many kings and the five Aryan tribes that were settled along its banks. These tribes had prospered for the fertile land along the course of Sarasvati. Details about the class structure of the Indus-Sarasvati Civilisation are not available. There is some evidence for slavery in the main labour quarters behind a large granary at Harappa. These labours might have been slave workers engaged either in temples or in municipality office. But the mechanism and intensity of violence are not known.

There is no evidence that the sturdy axes, knives of bronze which were found, were used as weapons. There were no swords at all. Arrowheads made of stone and the bow might have been used for hunting. No graves contained weapons. The spear-heads found are of thin and feeble copper. The implication is that religious systems were very strong and acted as a force in maintaining the class structure. This is supported by a few evidences that show the dead persons put into a sack lying in the middle of the street or on a stairway.

Land was territory, not property. Cattle had a common tribal brand, hence were held in common. The king was the leader of the war, president at the ritual sacrifice; symbol of tribal unity; apportioner of surplus within the tribe, and often elected to the highest position of the office.

The only private property was tools and weapons, though the traders used to accumulate precious metals. These tribes were not primitive, as they knew the rudiments of class structure. They held in varying numbers *sudras* and tribal *helots* whose surplus was property of the tribe as a whole.

The *sudras* and helots had not the right of initiation into the tribe. They did neither have any claim upon tribal property, nor a claim to their own surplus products. They might have been acquired by the rulers as a result of the conquest. The tribes also had a new type of priesthood barely mentioned as a separate caste in the *Rigveda*. They were brahmins, who recognised other tribes as their kins, often transcending tribal limits. However, the real castes were two, *arya* and *sudra,* the main class division without intermarriage. These tribes continued to exist in western Punjab till the time of Alexander (330 B.C.). The king Puru was descendant of these tribes.

The Rigvedic king used to receive voluntary sacrificial contributions from the tribes, not tribute exacted by force from them. This system created a new form of property in the hands of the king. For settlement of the land and for a greater surplus by cultivation, tribes used to contribute to the kings. In this way, it was possible for the kings to accumulate wealth. The five tribes are nowhere explicitly named in any early source. However, a set of five tribal names occurs in just one place in *Rigveda* (1.108.8). They were yadu, turvasa, anu, druhyu and puru. Each of these tribes is mentioned separately in other Rigvedic hymns. The first four come together again in *Rigveda* (8.10.5), which led to the conjecture that the seer belonged to the fifth, the purus. Turvasa is generally found with yadu and anu. Druhyu are comparatively rare. The purus were perhaps the most favoured single Rigvedic people though occasionally cursed by a hostile seer like Vasistha in the famous ten kings hymns in *Rigveda* (7.18). In that *sukta,* all five are among the many enemies over whom king Sudas prevailed, except the yadus who might perhaps be concealed under the little yaksu. But it is not clear whether the ruling class consisted of *priest-kings* or the *merchants,* described as the *panis* in the *Rigveda,* or a combination of both. At the same time, it is possible that the cultivating communities were of practically servile status – the *dasyus* or *dasas* of the *Rigveda.* Presence of slave labour in towns has indeed been deduced from archaeological remains.[1]

This class of tribes were divided into a large number of independent tribes, normally ruled by the kings, who, when not fighting with the *dasas* or dasyus, were frequently engaged in fighting each other. One such fighting was the battle of the ten kings mentioned in the *Rigveda* in the seventh mandala. Fighting was between various Vedic and non-Vedic tribes in the region of what is now Punjab near Parusni (Ravi) river. The conflict was between the bharata tribe led by king Sudas and a coalition of other tribes. King Sudas was victor of the battle and this led to the settlement by the puru-bharat tribe in the region which was near today's Kurukshetra. In this battle of ten kings, all the people of the Rigvedic India were involved. This battle is important as it heralded the spread of Vedic beliefs to other parts of the world, for the reason that the kings and their subjects were forced to pay tributes and had to migrate outwards towards the present lands now called as Iran, Iraq, Egypt.

Guided by the royal sage *Vishvamitra*, this army came on to oppose the bharata king Sudas in the battle. But, Sudas defeated them all, and captured all the Rigvedic tribes. Sudas's capital city was on the bank of Sarasvati river. He inherited the kingdom from his grandfather and greatly expanded it. He was supported by the spiritual mentorship of his guru, the legendary sage *Vasistha*. In the process, he alienated all the neighbouring kingdoms surrounding him. After years of subjugation, a group of a dozen or ten kings and chieftans formed a confederacy to combine their strength and defeated king Sudas once for all. Nevertheless, the people of Indus-Sarasvati Civilisation were highly conscious of their ethnic unity, based on a common language, a common religion, and a common way of life, and of the contrast between themselves and earlier inhabitants.

## Social Structure and Productive System

Social structure and productive system in the Indus-Sarasvati Civilisation are found from the philological research in the early

---

[1]  D. R. Chanana, Slavery in Ancient India: As Depicted in Pali and Sanskrit Texts, Delhi, 1960.

Indo-European languages and detailed textual studies of the *Rigveda*. The people obtained great mobility by domesticating horse. They were pastoralists. Cows and cattle were the main form of wealth. They combined pastoralism with agriculture. The use of the plough was known to them. Barley and some other cereals were the crops they grew in their early phase.[2] From the available evidences, it appears that people in this civilisation had, in the initial stages, a simple social structure. They were divided among tribes and lived in villages.

The *Rigveda* refers to three distinct classes: the *kshatriyas* or *rajanyas* (warriors, rulers), the *brahmanas* (priests) and the *vaisya* (masses).[3] The wealth of the first two classes was counted not in reference to land, but in reference to how many cows, horses, and slaves they owned.[4] The only payment to the kings was an offering rather than a tax.[5] The system was such that there was no over lordship of the land, vesting in either the tribal chief, the village-chief, or anyone else. Some references from the *Rigveda* indicate that private land ownership in the homestead and arable land had then existed, and that there was no communal ownership.[6]

Land was divided among fields cultivated by individual peasants who were regarded as the holders (kshetrapati) of the field. Pasture lands were apparently undivided and were open to the cattle of the whole village. Whether the right to the field was permanent or hereditary or subject to change by communal allotment cannot be established. At that time, cultivation was not settled but migratory. It was abundant. People were living so often

---

2    N. Bandyopadhyaya, Economic Life and Progress in Ancient India: Being the Outline of an Economic History of Ancient India, Calcutta, 1945.

3    N. Bandyopadhyaya, Economic Life and Progress in Ancient India, and R. S. Sharma, Sudras in Ancient India, Delhi, 1958.

4    N. Bandyopadhyayay, Economic Life and Progress in Ancient India, D. R. Chanana, Slavery in Ancient India and S. K. Das, Economic History of Ancient India.

5    U. N. Ghoshal, Contributions to the History of the Hindu Revenue System, Calcutta, 1929.

6    N. Bandyopadhyayay, Economic Life and Progress in Ancient India, Calcutta, 1945.

as semi-nomadic pastoralists. The conception of permanent occupation, or ownership of a particular portion of fields was not possibly developed. Some tribes used to cultivate the land in common. This practice probably continued in Punjab during the time of Alexander.[7]

The equalitarian structure of the agrarian society of the people of Indus-Sarasvati Civilisation was affected in course of time by their struggles with indigenous enemies[8]. The *dasas* were not all slaughtered; some were enslaved. Slaves, both male (*dasa*) and female (*dasi*), as mentioned in the *Rigveda* were like the desirable commodities to be obtained as gifts.[9] These slaves were, in course of time, absorbed in the mainstream[10]. These people were mostly city-dwellers. It is probable that the *sudra* class arose out of these population and brought under the rulers.[11] The *sudras* were recognised in the last portion of the *Rigveda* as the fourth *varna* placed beneath the class *vaisya*. There is no evidence as to the actual status of the *sudras* in the early Vedic period. It is, however, reasonable to suppose from various documents that they were not peasants. It might be that they were servile field-labourers for the tribes or for their individual masters, or were possibly helots.[12]

In a society, the class of peasants originates only when civilisation is established as a major source of income. Members of a family can then employ the major part of its labour-time on the cultivation. In this process, people from other professions join into this class. In Indus–Sarasvati valleys, the land was fertile. Much labour was not required to get food yield. So, peasants represented majority of entire population. During the period of this civilisation,

---

[7]    D. D. Kosambi, An Introduction to the Study of Indian History, Bombay, 1956.

[8]    R. S. Sharma, Sudras in Ancient India, Delhi, 1958.

[9]    Ibid.

[10]   D. D. Kosambi, An Introduction to the Study of Indian History, Bombay, 1956.

[11]   R. S. Sharma, Sudras in Ancient India, Delhi, 1958.

[12]   D. D. Kosambi, An Introduction to the Study of Indian History, Bombay, 1956.

monogamistic family evolved as a basic unit of society. Mesolithic communities who consumed wild rice, belonged to the pre ISC period. Agriculture as a profession and domestication of animals came into being with the neo-lithic revolution.

Two zones where crops were raised have been identified. The first is in the Belan valley (Kodihwa and Mahagara) where grains of cultivated rice and bones of domesticated cattle, sheep and goats have been found for the period 6500 to 4500 B.C. The second zone is that of the Kachhi plain, south of the Bolan Pass – an arid area, but experiencing seasonal floods from hill Torrents.

Remains of barely, corn-wheat, emmer and bread-wheat have been found in Mehragarh. Bones of wild animals, domestic cattle, sheep and goats were also found. These remains are of seventh to fourth millennium B.C.[13] Agriculture and domestication of cattle marked a notable stage in human progress, though method of farming was of primitive type. There was no use of the plough to improve yield-seed ratio. There could only be one cropping season. Area of the cultivated land were not large for absence of tools for clearing the dense forests and making the land suitable for cultivation. Internal structure of these crop-raising communities could not be assessed. Cultivation was only for gathering food with women as the principal workers[14]. Men used to go for hunt, and later on, tend cattle for meat and milk.

Sexual division of labour was not sufficient to produce a surplus which could create any class division or even occupational stratification. Evidences are there for existence of hoe-using neo-lithic community during sixth millennium B.C. During this period, there was probably social equalitarianism.[15]

During the later part of ISC, though the method of cultivation continued on plough cultivation, ox was used both for cultivation

---

[13]  N. D. N. Sahi's paper *'Early History of Agriculture in Pre- and Proto-Historic India'*, Indian History Congress, Bodhgaya, 1981. The Belan evidence is now held to be dubious.

[14]  V. Gordon Childe, *Man Makes Himself,* London, 1948.

[15]  Walter A. Fairservis, Jr. *This Threshold of Civilization: An Experiment in Prehistory*, New York, 1975.

and as a draught animal for pulling the bullock cart. The discovery of the furrows of ploughed field at Kalibangan has indicated that plough was used to a large extent during ISC for cultivation of agricultural land. Besides use of wheat, rice, barley and bajra millets, evidences are there for use of sesame, a species of brassica, and oilseeds.[16]

The most remarkable crop was cotton, the earliest of industrial crops[17]. Production of multiple crops shows that the two-harvest system was gradually established and agriculture was accepted as a full-time occupation. Presence of a peasantry as a social class was strongly recognised. Full-fledged agriculture created enough surplus. The surplus created a class who accumulated wealth. This class started commanding on others. They developed social and administrative organisation[18].

Finally, the control over bronze, an expensive metal, could give a small town-based class an effective sway over a mass of stone-tool-using peasantry. Social structure created by these material circumstances was followed by religion of gods, superstitions and emergence of priests. Development of agriculture, the creator of agrarian economy thus caused emergence of a differentiated society. The ISC not only gave Indian subcontinent its first peasantry, but also the concept of towns and cities, town planning, municipal laws and the way of comfort living. The way the cities were planned indicated high degree of political, judicial and administrative order[19].

There were only a few large cities. Other settlements were few and small, scattered from the Rann of Kutch to Simla and Bikaner. They were much thinner than those in Sumer or Babylon. Precious objects still found in the ruins and massive structure of the houses prove that a few people possessed huge wealths.

There were no great palace or monuments, or great temples in

---

[16] Sir John Marshall, Mohenjodaro and the Indus Civilization, London, 1931.

[17] Ibid.

[18] Sir George Watt, Commercial Products of India, London, 1908.

[19] V. Gordon Childe, What Happened in History, revised edition, 1954.

the city. The traders' seals show exclusively male animals and a three-faced God, similar to Shiva. The traders were thus men with their own property. They were the *panis* of the *Rigveda* as against the general country population, the *dasa* or *dasyu*. Pottery is found in very large quantities at all ancient sites. It was regarded as the index to the economic and artistic standard of the population of ISC. These are reflected in the remains of a few sculptural or other artistic pieces that still survive. The terracotta figurines, human as well as animal, show vigour, variety, and ingenuity.

During Indus-Sarasvati Civilisation, literacy was much improved compared to the status in the Rigvedic period. During the Rigvedic period, people were used to learning by hearing, but in Indus-Sarasvati Civilisation, they knew writing. And *Rigveda* has no allusions to artistic iconography, like, paintings, relic representations, statues or seals which were common in the Indus-Sarasvati Civilisation.

## Trade and Commerce

During the period of ISC, no great monuments like the pyramids were built. The rulers focused on town planning, civic amenities, comfort and sophisticated way of living. During this period of civilisation, people used to do maritime trading business. Western India was at that time much wetter than it is today. Monsoon rain was heavy which used to continue for a longer time. Rann of Kutch used to receive fresh water from both Sarasvati and Indus. The estuary of the Indus and Sarasvati was much further east than it is today. Scientific studies reveal that Indus used to enter the Arabian sea through the fortress of the semi-abandoned town of Lakhpat which still stands today.

Sea level during that time was several metres higher than it is today. Saurashtra peninsula was an island. Ships could comfortably sail through what are now the salt flats and marshes of the Rann of Kutch to make their way out to the gulf of Cambay. A port was built at Dholavira in the third millennium B.C. The place was on a strategically located island. It was accessible by boat from the Arabian sea to the west as well as the gulf of Cambay to the south. Boats from Dholavira could sail through both Indus and Sarasvati rivers and reach the cities that were located along their banks.

Thus, Dholavira had served as a very important place for commercial and military purposes.

The same is true for Lothal. When the course of Sutlej shifted east-ward and Yamuna shifted south-ward due to tectonic movement of plates of Indian subcontinent, Sarasvati river was deprived of perennial glacial water. Intensity of rainfall also diminished due to climate change. As a result, the courses of Sarasvati river became gradually non-navigable all the way to Dholavira. Large and complex urban centres flourished as did ports strung along more than 1000 kilometres of coast between Sutkagen-gor on the gulf of Oman and Lothal on the gulf of Cambay. Such ports were served by the immediate hinterland of the fertile Indus–Sarasvati valley and by overland trade routes linking the valley to Baluchistan and Afghanistan.

While some of the goods traded out of the Indus–Sarasvati valley may have comprised raw materials, such as, timber, semi-precious stones and ivory, exports also comprised manufactured goods. The weaving of cotton cloth was pioneered in the Indus–Sarasvati valley and traders from its cities sold cotton cloth and worked glass and shell beads in the markets of Mesopotamia, travelling in coastal vessels via Oman and Dilmun (Bahrain) from where copper and pearls were obtained. Return cargoes may have carried woollen cloth and similar items produced by the skilled artisans of many cities sustained by the waters of the Tigris and Euphrates.[20]

Around 2000 B.C., overland routes through the mountains of Baluchistan and across the Iranian highlands, provided a link between the civilisations of Mesopotamia and the ISC. Although the type of goods traded along these routes are not known, there are clues indicating a movement of people and cultures between these two areas. Similarly, there were overland routes which linked the Indus–Sarasvati valley people to the Hindu Kush and Afghanistan.

The river system was the main trade route. Trade formed an

---

[20]  S. Ratnagar, Encounters: Westerly Trade of the Harappa Civilization, 1981; M. K. Dhavalikar, 1991.

important part of city life. Mesopotamian imports are found in the Indus cities. Indus seals and products are found in Mesopotamia. There was, in fact, a stratum common to the ISC and Sumerian civilisation. This trade led to considerable accumulation of wealth by a few people. There was not overall development all over the areas under ISC.

## End of Indus-Sarasvati Civilisation

By 1700 B.C. it is believed that this civilisation started decaying, possibly due to factors like climate changes, shift of tectonic plate resulting in the change in the course of the rivers. According to the scholars, Indus-Sarasvati Civilisation had gone through three phases. The earliest recognisable site on the bank of Sarasvati was near Bhirrana in Haryana. From scientific evidence, it was found that the site was carbonated to 7000 B.C. From around 5000 B.C. the monsoon which was heavy around 7000 B.C. started gradually weakening. The first phase lasted till about 2600 B.C. The second phase lasted from 2600 to 2000 B.C. This was the period that witnessed the rise of major cities like Mohenjodaro, Harappa, Dholavira, Kalibangan, Lothal and so on. Some of these settlements which already existed in the previous phase expanded substantially.

Results of recent excavations suggested that the largest of these cities was near Rakhigarhi in Haryana, which was in the Sarasvati-Ghaggar basin. Archaeological evidence showed a steady decline after 2000 B.C. Cities were abandoned. Civic management deteriorated. There were signs of economic stress. The third phase of Indus-Sarasvati Civilisation petered out by 1400 B.C.

Experts of the Indus-Sarasvati Civilisation examined all the paleo-environmental and geological data relevant to Sarasvati river. They concluded that the river could have flowed down to the ocean only before 3200 B.C. at the very latest, preferring a date close to 3800 B.C. They are of the opinion that Sarasvati river stopped flowing into the ocean around 1900 B.C. after going through many stages of desiccation.

# A Journey to find the Source of Sarasvati

## In Search for the Source

Arko becomes more serious when it comes to Aditi's well being. Days have passed after Arko completed his studies on the three topics that Aditi wanted to know. Aditi was happy with the seriousness and sincerity with which Arko did his job. And now, Aditi only wants to see the source of Sarasvati river.

'Sarasvati is calling me…can't you hear her call?' Aditi murmurs for the thousandth time a day. She has no other notion of thought in her mind. One day, Arko looked at her, astonished. Her face has taken on phantasmagoric appearance, heightened by the rays of a strange light. She returned her gaze coldly.

Aditi's parents got worried. Finally they decided to allow Arko and Aditi for a trip to visit Adibadri and Bandarpoonch.

Aditi's father has collected a lot of information from various sources and from a few travel agents having specialised guide for trekking in high altitude mountain.

'Located in the Uttarkashi district of Uttarakhand, Bandarpoonch is a major peak of the Garhwal division of the Himalayas. The peak's name literally means *Tail of the monkey*. Yamunotri, the source of the river Yamuna is located on a flank of the Bandarpoonch peak. A long stretch of Bandarpoonch glacier feeds water to the Yamuna. Yamunotri glacier, Sworgarohini peak and Kalanag peak are around Bandarpoonch massif and its glacier'. Aditi gives a nod as his father narrates it.

She says, 'According to Hindu mythology, Lord Shiva came on Earth in the form of a monkey to test the strength of Bheema and sat leisurely spreading his tail from Hanuman Chatti to

Bandarpoonch. Bheema, proud of his strength, tried to remove the long-spread tail out of his way but was not able to do so. He realised that the monkey was not a normal monkey. He then surrendered to Lord Shiva.'

Aditi asks his father, 'Tell us if you have collected other information about Bandarpoonch and Adibadri.'

'The Bandarpoonch massif has three mountain peaks. The twin peaks of Banderpoonch I and Bandarpoonch II and Kalanag peak. These peaks can easily be spotted from many places in Garhwal. The first successful expedition to Bandarpoonch was led by Maj Gen Harold Williams in 1950 with a team comprising of legendary mountaineer Tenzing Norgay. This mountain rose to prominence when the Doon school masters Jack Gibson and John Martyn started using this area to offer climbing experience to their wards during the summer holidays. They were the first ones to actually reconnoiter the route in 1937. Tenzing Norgay refers to Bandarpoonch as The Doon School Mountain in his autobiography. One can approach the mountain from the south east route; the same route which was used for successful climbing for the first time by Nehru Institute of Mountaineering in 1975 when it took its students of Advance Mountaineering Course in the spring season. The trek to base camp starts from Sukhi, which lies on the road going up to Gangotri', Aditi's father takes a pause.

'What about Adibadri?' Aditi enquires from her father.

'Adibadri is a group of sixteen temples, located close to Karnaprayag. The main temple is dedicated to Lord Vishnu and a part of the famous Panch Badri pilgrimage circuit. The Panch Badris are: Badrinath, Bhavishya Badri, Yogdhyan Badri, Vridh Badri and Adibadri. Seven temples of this chain were built during the late Gupta period between fifth century to eighth century A.D. It is also believed that Lord Vishnu used to live here in Satya, Treta and Dwapar Yugas. In Kali Yug, he shifted to Badrinath. That is why this place is known as Adribadri. These temples were sanctioned by Adi Shankaracharya who wanted to spread the tenets of Hinduism to every remote corner of the country', her father narrates.

After three days, Arko and Aditi take a flight for Delhi. Flight was late, but they reached on apposite time. They had a bite together at the airport restaurant prior to going to the hotel. After taking lunch they went to the Indian archaeological museum and were happy to see the models, some ruins and some statues. Aditi's mind searches for old idols of Sarasvati. For the moment's bliss, she becomes dumbfounded. She finds the idols of Sarasvati of various sizes. She buys one and keeps it in her knapsack.

'Pretty but not very practical', says Arko, 'It can break during our journey'.

Aditi becomes furious. She retorts, 'It is not going to break. And I am going to leave it at the emerging spot of Sarasvati river at Adibadri. And please remember, it is our pilgrimage, not a journey.'

From Delhi they come to Dehradun by overnight train. The train journey was smooth, but they had spent a sleepless night on the train – the result of a sense of apprehension about what was going to happen once they reach Bandarpoonch and Adibadri. They checked in a hotel at Dehradun. In the afternoon, they were standing by the hotel window. Colour of the sunlight reflected on the window was light brown like the hazel-nut.

'Why are you always looking up in the sky? What do you find there?' Arko asks softly.

'Solace', replies Aditi swiftly. Her attire, her way of talking and every steps that she takes are so inviting that she seems to be like Goddess Sarasvati. Aditi shakes her bangles and touches Arko's face. Arko feels the sensation it creates. They walk across the courtyard which is spic and span and sit on a bench holding each other's hand.

'Arko, we are not far off from our reach.'

'Yes Aditi, as soon as we reach Uttarkashi, our guide will meet us and take us to Sukhi. From there trekking will start. Do not worry.'

'I am not worried. I am excited', Aditi grins at Arko with mischievous smile.

'Arko, let's go for a walk, I feel like walking'.

Arko smiles and takes her hand, 'I am more excited than you

are, but I try to keep me calm and quiet. Reaching upto the source of Sarasvati is not an easy trek.'

'You are with me. So I am full of energy', Aditi presses Arko's cheek.

'I know you are also with me,' Arko asserts.

When they are about to cross the courtyard, an old woman turns to Aditi and, without even asking who we are, tells us with delicate gesture to follow her to the reception of the hotel. Then, in a kind of trance, placing the palms of her hand on Aditi's head, says, 'May the Goddess Sarasvati be with you, and may she show you the only thing that you need to discover; may you walk neither too slowly nor too fast but always according to the laws and the requirement of the trek; may you obey the one who is your guide, even though he may issue an order that is homicidal, blasphemous, or senseless. You, must swear total obedience to your guide.'

Having said this, she returns to her normal manner.

'She has been sent to me by Sarasvati', Aditi murmurs.

At the night, they had a sound sleep. Next day early morning, they start for Uttarkashi. They reached there before noon. They checks in a guest house whose owner is one of Arko's friends. It is on a spot bounded by a mountain to the south and an even higher mountain to the north. Between them the undulating, green hilly terrain. Amidst the rising and falling landscape is a small area of level land where the guest house is located. Everywhere there are cardamom plants, scent of flowers. All over spread thick the Davana scented leaves, intoxicating the viewer by stimulating his memory. Their aroma coils the belly of the mountains.

'My enthusiasm is at the peak, an enthusiasm to penetrate and live in a new world. I feel like shouting in elation', Aditi exclaims.

Arko says, 'Aditi, do you know what bliss shines in your face?'

'I don't need to say it to you. I feel it as I watch the surrounding blue, climbing up and down, winding round the mountainous terrain. I feel like piercing the sky with a stick', Aditi cries out with emotion.

Madhu, the guesthouse-keeper welcomes them with soup,

spicy bread and chicken korma. These mountain people have diverse taste for food.

'I live in nearby quarter', says Madhu', 'Call me if you ever need anything. I am leaving now.'

In the evening, their guide meets them and finalises the itinerary.

An old lady serves them with organic food which is delicious. Madhu arranges some wood and dry leaves to create a camp fire at night.

'We must reach the peak of Bandarpoonch massif. Sarasvati is calling me' says Aditi with her sparkling eyes, 'I hear her inner voice – the babbling noise of her flowing water.'

The next day they start for Bandarpoonch massif. Everything is covered under a white layer of snow.

They get on the Arakote-bound bus with four porters and the guide at half past five in the morning. The bus runs through the Tamasa valley. There are very few ups and downs. The bus reaches *Purola* via Brahmakhal and Barkote. The river Tamasa flows by the side of the road. The guide says, 'Tamasa valley is the land of the Kauravas. The people residing in this valley worship Duryodhana, the eldest brother of the Kauravas, as their deity. Bhogdatta, one of the soldiers who fought on the side of the Kauravas in the war of Kurukshetra came to this region and settled permanently. Since then adoration of Duryodhana had started without a break.'

Seeing a temple of Duryodhana in Purola, Aditi enquires, 'Is there similar temple elsewhere?'

'Statues of Duryodhana can be seen in various villages of this region. The fair is held in sequences in every village when the deity of Duryodhana is brought there', answers the guide.

Crossing *Purola*, the road is on the left side of Tamasa river which flows much below the road level. Here the river is calm, pleasant and flows with a poetical metre. Aditi looks at the river with fixed eye in a mood of indifference. The river Tamasa does not disappear from their eyes even for a moment. At two o'clock, the bus reaches a small town, named *Sori*. They get out of the bus for a break.

The bus then starts for a long way to Arakote along the left side of Tamasa. The next destination is *Sankri* via *Naitiyar*. Within an hour, the bus reaches *Naitiyar*. The river Tamasa emerges from Naitiyar as a result of the union of two drains - Rupin and Supin. The river Rupin comes from Himachal Pradesh. So the river Supin now becomes their companion for the rest of the journey.

After *Natiyar*, they enter the protected forest called *Govinda Pashu Bihar*. The officer of the forest department gives the permit in the bus. They reach *Sankri* at seven in the evening and check in the forest department's bunglow there.

Looking at the people sitting here and there, Aditi tells Arko, 'It appears that the people over here do not get proper food and clothes'.

The guide clarifies, 'The economic condition of the inhabitants of some parts of the Himalayas is comfortable. But the picture in this remote zone is completely different. Far from being comfortable, poverty has gripped them on all sides. Farming is the only profession. If there is less rain in any year, the economic condition becomes precarious. The inhabitants in such remote places are to fight against thousands of adversities. Besides, the beasts of the forest often destroy their crop and they do not get any compensation from the government for the damage. The financial situation is so miserable that the young boys carry the luggage of tourists weighing twenty five to thirty kilos for three days for a paltry sum of five hundred rupees.'

Aditi is tender-hearted. She informs with modesty to the guide, 'We shall pay to the porters much more that amount'. The guide appreciates with radiant face.

The expedition starts at half past nine next day. The target site of the first day is *Taluka*. The distance is thirteen kilometers. On both sides of the trek there is dense forest. Road is smooth. They cross three connecting canals - Hallargarh, Bingad and Giagad. They reach the village Taluka at noon. The guide has made the arrangement for their stay at a beautiful bunglow in the center of the Taluka village which is at about six and a half thousand feet altitude.

The next morning they pack up and start walking again. The destination is to reach the village called *Seema*. The river Supin is on the left side of the route. The path is much narrower with more acclivity and declivity. The river Supin suddenly disappears and then reappears soon. Observing Supin's hide-and-seek game, they reach the destination in the evening. Here also they stay in the government bunglow. *Seema* is the last village on this route. Height is about eight and a half thousand feet. There are only a few houses in this village. Just on the other side of the river Supin, there is another village named *Osla*. This village is famous for grazing ground for cattles. From *Seema* one can go to 'Har-Ki-Dun'. Several peaks of the Himalayas are seen from this place.

Next day they are to trek a long way. So, they leave before eight o'clock. Here, Supin canal is divided into two parts – 'Har-Ki-Dun' flows on the left side of the route, the other one - Ruisara canal flowing on the right side. The trek is through deep forest leaving Ruisara canal on the left. The trek is with steep ascent. Within two hours, they arrive at a wide flat land known as *Rupsa*. Spacious pastures. From here, they first see the peak of Krishnachura. After crossing the pastures, they descend straight down to the shore of Ruisara canal crossing a wooden bridge. They begin to move forward. No more climbing. Grandeur of flowers of different colours. These colourful environment does not allow anyone to feel the fatigue for trekking. A number of waterfalls have descended through the stone walls on the opposite side. Finally, they arrive in the evening at the *Ruisara Tal,* the main camp of their expedition. The place is about twelve and a half thousand feet altitude.

Swargarohini mountain is in the east; Jamunetri Pass is in the west; the road to Hanumanchati is in the north and Bandarpoonch is in the south. In the middle of them is the Ruisara lake. The guide decides to set up the camp at Kiyarkoti which is about 14,000 feet altitude.

Arko and Aditi decides to take rest in the tent set up at this place. A young hill man comes to them immediately after they enter the tent.

'Hello Saheb, I am Kebal Singh. Do you know where has my brother who has come with you as a porter gone?'

'No, we don't know. But why do you want to know?', Aditi asks.

'His marriage ceremony has been held today in the morning. I have come to give this news to him.'

'How come his marriage ceremony has been held while he is with us?' Aditi enquires.

'Our rule is that a girl is married to all the brothers. The family of the bridegroom give dowry to the bride's family and this is compulsory. The amount is also huge. Moreover, a girl is married many times. The dowry received on account of her first marriage goes to the girl's father and thereafter, her ex-husbands get the share of the dowry. In some area of this region, with the birth of the daughter, the father gets the dowry in advance and when the daughter attains the marriageable age, they get married after receipt of the rest of the dowry. In the hilly region, girls do not have their own opinion on any issue. So, this system is only for selling the girl indirectly.'

Aditi offers him rice with raw onion and jam jelly. Sitting in front of the tent with absolute satisfaction, the boy finishes his wedding lunch!

## Arko Rediscovers Aditi

Next day, they leave this place and start for the camp of Kiarkoti. They cross the ascent upto Bugiyal and then reach the south-western slope of Swargarohini. After trekking southwards for an hour, they turn left at right angle along the slope. Below is the source of Ruisara canal. From there they finally come down to Bandarpoonch glacier just above the source of Ruisara canal. Leaving the middle line of the glacier on the right, they start walking on the glacier taking the rocky path.

'Come on Aditi, we are at the point wherefrom Sarasvati emerged long ago', Arko exclaims.

The weather suddenly gets worse. The snow begins to fall and lasts until evening.

The next morning, there were no signs of bad weather. The path is unfamiliar and relatively difficult along the southwest ridge.

Unknown inaccessible path. The steepness is about seventy degrees. Three-point climbing has to be done in many places. They do not find a place to rest. Just a wall of ice in front of the eyes. Nothing more can be seen.

Now they are close to the mountain peak, but they do not get any energy. 'What to do?, Arko enquires in a tremulous voice.

'I feel a chill inside. We have been travelling since long. How long any idea? For six to seven days, I suppose. Any idea where are we heading towards?', Aditi's voice was trembling. They still do not stop. The two young souls travels and trek up in white.

Amidst this coldest journey, Aditi starts breathing heavily. Her arms are tangled with Arko's arms.

Aditi suddenly says, 'Arko, I find swans hovering over my head. Can't you see them? Is it an illusion or reality?' Aditi keeps her eyes open.

The guide understands the situation. He tells them to wait there for some time.

Seeing the condition of Aditi, the guide advises them to stop climbing further.

Aditi breaks down and says, 'No! So near yet so far! I'll be going upto the source of the river.'

Having come all the way from Kolkata to this place to see the source of Sarasvati river – the river that can light up the life of Aditi, Arko does not agree to stop climbing.

Arko realises the sorrow of Aditi. The guide tells Arko to climb along with him and requests Aditi to wait at that place. Aditi starts crying 'No Arko…I'm not weak, I'll go with you.'

Arko softly holds her hands and they start climbing again. There comes a point when they reach almost to the peak.

There is no sign of any river, but the place is truly an enchanting and serene atmosphere. Arko finds the sun has began to set on the western horizon. From the crimson – red hue, the sun is slowly turning yellow saffron and then it finally plunges beneath the horizon. In the midst of this silent drama of changing hues Arko looks at Aditi's face. The face looks like milky white. Arko finds one swan sitting on the top of the peak. He sees Aditi sitting on the white swan in a beautiful white saree with a border of gold. Arko seems to see the figure of a serene Sarasvati. She is gazing at him, with her palm raised in the *abhyamudra* and blessing him with a smile. And caressing the slope of the glacier, the Sarasvati is flowing silently.

Arko hears as if Aditi is saying – 'Arko, you have kept your promise by coming to this sacred place. You have seen me too in the Sarasvati. I am fulfilled'. Arko was unaware about how long he had spent in this reverie drenched with Aditi. Arko feels someone is standing beside him. He opens his eyes and Aditi says, 'Perhaps that is the end of your pilgrimage. Here is hot tea. Please drink it'. Never before had such hot tea tasted so delicious. Having finished with it, Arko puts his arms around Aditi and says, 'Aditi, there is a part of Mother Sarasvati inside you. You will one day find out the truth of your existence'. Aditi smiles and says, 'Let us go and climb down the foothill.'

# Sarasvati appears at Adibadri

## New Beginnings

After taking two days' rest, Arko and Aditi start for Adibadri via Karnaprayag. Reaching there they meet the local people. The locals have multiple views regarding the existence of Sarasvati river. According to some of the aged people Sarasvati exists and is known as *Ikshumati*. They find some water channels. The local people consider these channels to be the part of Sarasvati river. Whole year several festivals are organised in the name of the Sarasvati river. They come to know that after coming to power in Haryana in October 2014, the BJP-led Haryana government has announced its intent to revive the mythical river. Among the various works proposed to be undertaken are the construction of Adibadri dam on *Somb* river and its piped link to the origin of the Sarasvati river and the proposed Sarasvati reservoir.

They meet an aged sadhu with huge beard.

'Do you know anything about the Sarasvati river?' Aditi asks.

'These channels are Sarasvati river', the sadhu tells them with confidence and then disappears.

They sit beside one water channel. The sadhu reappears there suddenly with his smoky eyes and tangled hair. The sadhu in a mesmerised voice tells them, 'Look at the channel'.

Arko and Aditi got surprised to find two lotuses floating in the channel.

'Pluck up the lotus and take a bath in this placid water.' Sadhu's voice reaches to them.

They take a bath and rise up from the water with lotus in hand.'

The sadhu, on all a sudden, bowes to them. He calls Aditi as

Sarasvati and starts moving fast.

Arko and Aditi get astounded.

They try to catch him with an intent to talk to him. But they fail to find him.

With heavy heart Arko and Aditi return to the hotel.

Aditi is silent but smiles at Arko. 'I told you something would happen.'

'I knew it even before you imagined', says Arko.

'Arko, I will be back at this place someday. I will continue my further research on the river Sarasvati.'

They smilingly walk towards Mantra devi temple. They pray for each other secretly.

Arko looks at Aditi and says, 'You know Aditi, I'll bring you again and again in this place, I have discovered a new YOU in this alluring journey.'

## A Dream for a Time Travel

*Life begins to end*

*Dreams are doors to valleys*

*Where tears flow to fertile lands...*

Arko was in a deep sleep when he heard Aditi whispering to his ears.

'Arko, wake up. It's time. I must leave! Wake up my love...'

He could see nothing when he opened his eyes, or perhaps he thought that he had opened his eyes. Aditi was nowhere, instead he could hear a distinct music of Veena. And he could feel the cold moisture, and it was clear that the river was very close to them. Arko tried to look around to call Aditi and tell her that they had been finally successful, but she was nowhere. There was only a darkness and a light that played hide and seek with his senses. He could sometimes hear a voice like Aditi's saying, 'I must leave!'

Arko went to Aditi's room. But she was not there. He went to the reception. No one had seen her. Arko called everyone they knew in that place. He was breathing hard.

An old woman was passing by him. Seeing him, she stopped. Arko looked at her. She did not smile, but said, 'The river. It called her.'

'What?' Arko was breathless.

The old woman got scared and she walked away.

'Hey! Hey you? Wait.' Arko ran after her. He stopped her.

She looked scared.

'What? What did you say?'

The old woman said nothing, she kept staring at him. The guide came running to Arko and said, 'Sir, let her go. She is insane.'

Arko was reluctant.

'Sir, please. Sir, I have news.'

'What? Where is she?'

The guide was quiet.

'Tell me...'

The guide took Arko to the water channel that was flowing through that place.

'What are we doing here?'

'Sir, they saw her last night.' The guide pointed to a group of children sitting on the bank of the channel. Arko was baffled, a voice came back to him – 'Wake up my love, I must go.' He rushed to the children and asked what they had seen.

'Mother goddess!' They chanted together.

'What?' Arko was feeling sick.

The guide said, 'Sir, they are very poor and uneducated. They may have seen or maybe...'

Arko went closer to them and asked, 'What did you see? Tell me and I will give you money.'

'No money! Mother goddess blessed us. We will go to school

and we will have good homes...'

Arko had difficulty in understanding their language, accent and broken english, The guide explained. Arko asked him, 'Who is the mother goddess?'

'Mother Sarasvati. We call her mother goddess.'

Arko almost fell on the ground. He looked at the channel, which was flowing silently. The guide said that the children usually played near the river at night since they had nothing else to do when their parents were out working or fighting with each other, and they had claimed that the night before they had heard the music of Veena and they had gone near the river. They had seen the most spectacular scene and they knew that they were blessed.

Suddenly Arko saw thousands of people coming towards the river. He asked, 'Who are they?'

'The people of these childrens' clans, sir. As I was telling you, they think that their civilisation is blessed again by the mother goddess like millions of years ago. Their children saw her last night, on a white dancing swan.'

Arko could not believe anything of what he heard. He said, 'I don't understand. Where is my Aditi? And what does all this nonsense have to do with her?'

'Sir, please listen,' The guide said in a calm tone. 'Aditi madam was a special soul.'

'Was?'

'Sir, the children had seen Aditi madam last night. She had somehow transformed and merged with the channel.'

Arko cried out. 'Have you lost your mind? Tell me where is Aditi? Did she get kidnapped? Are you involved?'

'Please sir. Please calm down.'

Arko sat on the bank of the channel. He couldn't speak. He called Aditi's number again and again. No one picked up. It rang, and rang. He called their parents and told what he was witnessing. He urged them to inform the police. And then it happened. He called Aditi's number again and this time he could hear the phone ringing. The guide could hear it too and he was surprised himself. It was ringing nearby, and then a little girl came to Arko.

'For you.' She handed Aditi's phone to Arko.

Arko almost fainted, 'Where, where did you find it?'

'Mother Goddess said that someone would call her. And I have the duty to give him the phone.'

Everything looked strange. There were thousands of people on the bank. The media and police reached. People were worshipping on the bank, people were praying to the water of the channel and to their ancestors. He looked for Aditi. Where could she be hiding? The police came, they assured that they would do their best to find her. The media took interviews. But Aditi was nowhere. There was an emptiness in Arko's heart.

And then he saw it. The little girl was still sitting beside him. The guide was sitting there too. Arko found a video. Aditi's last video.

'Arko, I had to do this. I know we love each other. But something is beyond our love and that is life. I am sorry, but I had no choice. Since the day we came on this expedition, I had been dreaming of strange things. I wanted to share with you, but I lacked words to describe the visions. Sometimes I wonder, what if I had listened to you and stayed back home. What if I had married you and created our own life? Then perhaps, we could have saved my human form in this birth. We were born in each era to prove love, and beyond that to prove the worth of life and even the greatest purpose of our births had been to save humanity from doom. Arko, I did not leave you. I will wait for you again.'

And there he saw her sitting at the bank of the same channel and crying. She was crying like a little child; she was transforming into a light, or was he imagining. There was nothing. The phone had nothing else to show. The little girl was still sitting at his feet and looking straight at him. Arko did not like her, yet he asked, 'What is your name?'

She got up, smiled and ran away; while running she looked back and said, 'Sarasvati.'

Arko could hear Aditi's voice somewhere around that place, and for no reasons at all he suddenly remembered Brahmā and Sarasvati, sitting on two lotuses in their holy abode and laughing together. Sarasvati was telling him about her wish to travel in time and create spaces for humans to explore the mysteries of life, while Brahmā was sharing with her the possibilities that the Universe holds. The discussion continued and Brahmā all of a sudden expressed his desire to love her, to which she laughed and belittled him.

Brahmā said, 'In all matters I have created you and so I keep the right to love you too!'

Sarasvati replied, 'Creation is always independent of its creator. You are changing the rule...'

Brahmā answered, 'There is no rule. I adore you...'

Sarasvati said, 'It is nothing but your limitless lust...'

Brahmā smiled and said, 'Only such a deep desire can bring progeny on Earth.'

Silence.

He tried to touch her, and immediately she disappeared. Her voice echoed through the emptiness of the Universe, 'I shall not believe you until you find me in each birth that I am going to take from this moment to teach you the value of a creation. In that process, I will visit the Earth each time to procreate ideas, fertile lands, and generations of thoughtful human beings to keep the civilisations of mankind oscillating in the midst of this Brahmanda.

Was it a dream? Arko could not decipher.

# Foundation's Publications

1. Engineering and Technology in Ancient India
2. *New Discoveries About Vedic Sarasvati*
3. *Dhanurveda: The Vedic Military Science*
4. *Vedic Concordance (Four Vols. )*
5. *Vedic and Classical Sanskrit - A Contrastive Analysis of Phonological and Morphological Features*
6. *Vedic Meteorology: The Ancient Indian Science of Rainmaking*
7. *Vedic Theory of Origin of Speech*
8. *Researches into Vedic and Linguistic Studies.*
9. *Bhāratīya Kālaganaṇā Kā Vaijñānika evaṁ Vaiśvika Svarūpa*
10. *Jesus, the Christ was a Hindu*
11. *History and Origin of Mathematics*
12. *Indian Origin of Greece and Ancient world*
13. *India the Civiliser of the World*
14. *Yuga yugin Trigarta (Trigarta through Ages)*
15. *Vedic Microbiology*
16. *Revisiting the Roots of Judeo-Christianity*
17. *Tributes to Renaissance Rishi*
18. *Rishi Dayananda in the Eyes of the West*
19. *Yogavāsiṭha Mahārāmāyaṇa*, edited with English translation: 8 vols.
20. *Vālmīki Rāmāyaṇa*, edited with English Translation: 4 vols.
21. *Ṛgveda*, edited with English Translation: 4 vols.
22. *Sāmaveda*, edited with English Translation
23. *Yajurveda*, edited with English Translation
24. *Nature of Vedic Science and Technology*
25. *Science of Vedic Meters and Musical notes*
26. *Science and Technology in Mahabharata*
27. *Reviving the Age-old Historical Tradition of India*
28. *Vedic Farming*
29. *Psychology in Yoga Darshan*
30. *Rainmaking With the help of Yajna*
31. *Stepping into the 52nd Century*
32. *Weather Forecast in Vedic Times*
33. *Sanskrit the Original Source of English*
34. *An Introduction to Bhāratīya Kālaganaṇā*
35. *Somayāga: Vedic Process of Rainformation*
36. *Agniṣomīya Paśuyāga: Vedic Operation for Rainmaking.*
37. *Concordance of Vedic Mantras as per Ṛsis and Devatās. (Two vols.)*
38. *Concordance of Vedic Mantras as per Devatas and Risis. (Two vols.)*
39. *Vedic Concordance of a quarter part of a mantra (The revised, redited, and updated Devanāgarī version of Bloomfield's Vedic Concordance) 4 Vols*
40. *Concordance of Vedic Rishis and Devatas*
41. *Concordance of Vedic Devatā and Ṛsis*

## Vedic Science

A Quarterly Journal of Indian Foundation for Vedic Science dedicated to the  Vedic Sciences and Scientific Interpretation of Vedas and Allied Literature

## World Vedic Calendar

World Vedic Calendar is a *Sāyaṇa Pañcāṅga* (updated according to precession). First time in the history of Indian calendars the details of Vedic solar months and lunar months have been given. This calendar cites Indian Festivals as astronomical according to Sāyaṇa Pañcāṅga and as historical according to *Niryaṇa Pañcāṅga*.

The Books are avialble on all Amazon cites and foundation's website: www.vedicscience.net